AMAZING animals

Nature's Most Incredible Creatures

Clever Camouflagers
by Anthony D. Fredericks

Smart Survivors
by Sneed B. Collard III

Surprising Swimmers
by Anthony D. Fredericks

Tough Terminators
by Sneed B. Collard III

Weird Walkers
by Anthony D. Fredericks

NorthWord Press
Minnetonka, Minnesota
www.howtobookstore.com

NorthWord Press
5900 Green Oak Drive
Minnetonka, MN 54343
1-800-328-3895
www.howtobookstore.com

ISBN 1-55971-752-1 (hardcover)
ISBN 1-55971-753-X (hardcover with comb binding)
Printed in Malaysia

10 9 8 7 6 5 4 3 2 1

CONTENTS

Clever Camouflagers

About Camouflagers 10

Chameleons 12

Leaf insects 14

Pipefish 16

Servals 18

Casque-headed Frogs 20

Orchid Praying Mantises 22

Sea Dragons 24

Flying Geckos 26

Walking Sticks 28

Ptarmigans 30

Sargassum Fish 32

Living Stones 34

Protecting Clever Camouflagers 36

Internet Sites 159

Index 160

DEDICATION
To George DeSou—A very clever un-camouflager!

ACKNOWLEDGMENTS
A special note of thanks to all my students—who continue to examine, invent, and promote all the creative possibilities of non-fiction literature.

CONTENTS

Smart Survivors

About Survivors 40

Nudibranchs 42

Kangaroo Rats 44

Strangler Figs 46

Fireflies 48

Deep-Sea Vent Organisms 50

Polar Bears 52

Weaver Ants 54

Cleaner Wrasses 56

Snakes 58

Bucket Orchids 60

Poison Arrow Frogs 62

Human Beings 64

Protecting Smart Suvivors 66

Internet Sites 159

Index 160

DEDICATION
For Rich Moser, a fellow survivor in good times and bad.

CONTENTS

Surprising Swimmers

About Swimmers 70

Squids 72

Sea Snakes 74

Marine Iguanas 76

Backswimmers 78

Krill 80

Lampreys 82

Scallops 84

Guillemots 86

Devil Fish 88

Purple Sea Snails 90

Puffer Fish 92

Sea Otters 94

Protecting Surprising Swimmers 96

Internet Sites 159

Index 160

DEDICATION
For my daughter Rebecca—with love and pride.

ACKNOWLEDGMENTS
A special note of thanks to Paula Gilbert—the world's greatest children's librarian—
for her efforts in making this dream possible.

CONTENTS

Tough Terminators

About Predators 100

Tiger 102

Ladybird Beetle (Ladybug) .104

North Pacific Giant Octopus 106

Aplomado Falcon 108

Saltwater Crocodile 110

Community Spider 112

Great Barracuda 114

Pitcher Plant 116

Siphonophore 118

Gray Wolf 120

Dragonfly 122

Gray Whale 124

Protecting Tough Terminators 126

The Top Predator 127

Internet Sites 159

Index 160

DEDICATION
For Larry Pringle.
Everlasting thanks for your guidance, humor, and quest for a better world.

CONTENTS

Weird Walkers

About Walkers 130
Mudskippers 132
Millipedes 134
Tree Frogs 136
Ostriches 138
Hydras 140
Measuring Worms 142
Mangrove Trees 144
Starfish 146
Basilisk Lizards 148
Snails 150
Water Striders 152
Sloths 154
Protecting Weird Walkers .156
Internet Sites 159
Index 160

DEDICATION
For my son Jonathan—with love and admiration.

ACKNOWLEDGMENTS
Special thanks to Mary Fitzgibbons—librarian at the Dover Area Community Library—
whose unfailing assistance and engaging effervescence made this book a reality.

CLEVER CAMOUFLAGERS

NATURE'S **MOST AMAZING** ANIMALS

Anthony D. Fredericks

About Camouflagers

Chameleon

Have you ever played a game of "hide and seek"? Did you try to hide from the person who was "it" by standing behind a tree or scrambling underneath something? If you were "it," did some of your friends make noises or have brightly colored clothing that made it easy for you to find them?

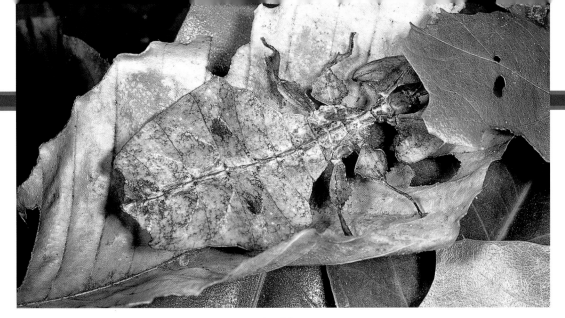

Leaf Insect

Many animals play "hide and seek" too, but for very different reasons. Some animals hide themselves to avoid being eaten by their enemies. Other animals disguise themselves so they can sneak up on their food and capture it. Scientists refer to this hiding ability as camouflage.

Several kinds of animals have colors or shapes that help them look like something else in their environment. There are fish, frogs, and insects that look just like leaves; grasshoppers that look like rocks or stones; moths and birds that resemble pieces of wood; lizards that look like trees or plants; and caterpillars that look like bird droppings.

Animals camouflage themselves for two reasons: to find food or to avoid becoming food for something else.

Scientists tell us that the colors and shapes of animals have come about (or evolved) over thousands or millions of years. An animal is able to survive because it has adapted to its environment—it knows how to locate its food and what to do to hide from its enemies. To do that some animals have developed distinctive means of camouflage—pretending to be something they are not.

In this book you will discover animals that play "hide and seek" every day of their lives. You'll learn about a bird that is white in winter and brown in summer, a frog that looks just like a leaf, a fish that looks like seaweed, and a lizard that changes its color a dozen times a day. For you, "hide and seek" may be a game; but for many animals, it is the only way they can survive.

CHAMELEONS

There are approximately 80 different species of chameleons throughout the world. These forest-dwelling animals live mostly in Africa, including the island nation of Madagascar, while a few species live in Arabia, India, and Ceylon.

Colorful Creatures

Stick out your tongue. How long is it? Like most people your tongue is probably 3 to 4 inches long. And, like most people, you use your tongue to help you eat and taste your food. What if your tongue were as long as your whole body and you could use it to capture your food and bring it into your mouth? That would be an incredible ability!

One amazing animal—the chameleon—not only has that wonderful skill, but also has another talent—one for which it is better known. In fact, when most people think about animals that are able to camouflage themselves, chameleons often come to mind.

As you may know, chameleons can change their body color to match their surroundings. For example, if a chameleon is resting on a green plant its skin color becomes green. If it is resting on a brown tree, its body color changes to brown.

A chameleon can change its color to shades of red or black as well.

Chameleons also change their skin color in response to the intensity of sunlight or the temperature of the air, or even their emotions. Not only do chameleons change their colors to blend in with their surroundings, they also do so to let other chameleons know how they feel.

Depending on the species, chameleons range in size from 2 inches to 2 feet long.

A chameleon's body is shaped like a leaf and ends in a prehensile (able to grasp objects) tail often held in a tight coil. Chameleons are very slow climbers, taking their time in moving through their environment.

One of the most distinctive features of a chameleon is its eyes—each of which can move independently from the other. Swiveling its eyes up and down lets the chameleon observe two separate objects at the same time or look at the same target from different angles. This ability is particularly handy when the chameleon looks for food.

Chameleons typically prey on insects, spiders, scorpions, and other small invertebrates (animals without backbones). Some of the larger species of

Fantastic Fact

If a chameleon loses a fight with another chameleon its skin turns dark green. If it is angry, its skin color changes to black.

chameleons, however, will attack small birds, mammals, and lizards. The chameleon is very patient. When it locates a potential meal it will look at it for some time before attacking.

Powerful muscles and a special bone in the chameleon's mouth make the attack quick. Its tongue shoots out, trapping the victim on the tip, and carries it back into the chameleon's mouth.

While this animal is one of nature's most unusual, it is also one in danger. Because it lives in the rain forests of the world, its habitat is being destroyed at an alarming rate. As the rain forests are being reduced, so is the chameleon's home. Saving the rain forests will help ensure its survival.

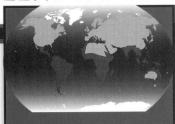

LEAF INSECTS

Leaf insects belong to a distinctive family of insects called Phasmids. Most of the members of this group of creatures inhabit forests and woodlands throughout the world—mostly in tropical regions. Many species can be found in the wooded areas of Australia and Southeast Asia.

Plant Pretenders

How would you like to be invisible, or almost invisible? How would you like to be able to sit in a classroom without being seen or walk through a shopping mall and not be noticed?

There is an insect that is practically invisible simply because it looks like a leaf. This extraordinary creature, the leaf insect, copies vegetation so closely that it is almost impossible to see, even when viewed close up. Since leaves are everywhere in the insect world, this characteristic has helped ensure the survival of this unique animal.

There are about 2,000 different species of leaf insects found throughout the world. They range in size from less than 1 inch to 1 foot long.

The eggs of leaf insects are hard-shelled and often look exactly like the seeds of the plants on which they feed. A female leaf insect will often lay hundreds of eggs a day. These eggs need four to six months before they hatch (depending on the temperature).

Young leaf insects are often marked and colored to look like glossy, green leaves. Their bodies are covered with branched vein patterns similar to those on a living leaf.

Occasionally, these animals have two or three brown spots on their bodies resembling the marks left on leaves by disease or the nibbling of other insects.

In fact, the appearance of young leaf insects matches their surroundings so closely that other animals can crawl right over them and not even know they are there.

Older and larger leaf insects also use color to camouflage themselves. As they mature, leaf insects turn brown, tan, or speckled in color—closely matching the colors of dead leaves scattered on the forest floor.

The limbs of these amazing creatures also resemble leaf parts. The legs and head are often shaped like flat extensions of a plant leaf or may even resemble the partially eaten parts of tree foliage (leaves).

During the day, leaf insects remain perfectly still for long periods of time. At night, however, they become active—seeking leaves and other vegetation. If startled by an approaching predator, a leaf insect can remain motionless for several hours looking just like every other leaf on the ground.

Flattened bodies, wings and legs with scalloped edges, green and brown coloring, and very slow movements allow this "plant pretender" to survive and thrive in a very hostile environment.

Fantastic Fact

Some species of leaf insects can change their color throughout the day—becoming light in the daytime and dark at night.

There are more than 150 different species of pipefish throughout the world. They can be found in the shallow waters of tropical and temperate seas, although a few live in depths of 50 feet or more.

Very Vertical Varieties

How long can you stand on your head? One minute? Two minutes? Five minutes? How do you think it would feel if you had to spend almost your entire life standing on your head? Well, you're about to meet a most unusual creature that does just that.

The pipefish is a slender fish with a long head and a **tubular** ("0"-shaped) mouth. Different species of pipefish range in size from 1 inch to 18 inches long.

**Unlike most fish,
pipefish can move
their eyes independently
of each other.**

Instead of scales, pipefish have a series of jointed bone-like rings encircling their bodies from their heads all the way down to the tips of their tails. These rings help pipefish maintain a pencil-like shape. Depending on the species, a pipefish's colors may range from bright green to drab olive.

Pipefish spend almost their entire lives swimming in a vertical (up and down) position. With their heads pointed toward the bottom of the ocean they look almost exactly like seaweed. Not only does this physical feature camouflage them from their enemies, it also allows them to

sneak up on their prey. Occasionally, however, pipefish do swim horizontally, especially if they need to escape an enemy.

Pipefish are related to sea horses; and they raise their young in similar ways. For example, some pipefish males have small pouches under their bellies in which the females lay eggs. In other species, the females lay their eggs on the underside of the males where they stick until hatching. Just like sea horses, the males typically take care of the young fish after they hatch.

Pipefish have no teeth, nor do they have a true mouth. Their jaws are locked into place—forming a permanent and unmovable opening. They eat by sucking small animals such as plankton directly into their stomachs.

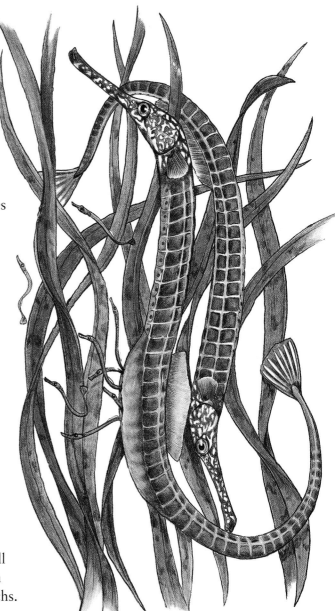

SERVALS

Servals can be found throughout Africa—particularly south of the Sahara Desert. They prefer to live in well-watered and open grassland areas of the continent.

Careful Creatures

Many animals have permanent markings, colors, or shapes that help them look like parts of the environment in which they live—a benefit in avoiding detection by their enemies. These animals take advantage of a biological feature known as protective coloration (skin or fur colorings which allow them to fade into the background and hide). This is particularly useful for young animals that are not strong enough or fast enough to escape their enemies.

One animal that exhibits this remarkable trait is the serval, a member of the cat family. At first glance, this animal appears to be a miniature cheetah. It has long legs, just like a cheetah, which help it move quickly through tall grass and swampy land. Its very large ears, which can turn in many different directions, help it locate the sounds of nearby animals. These features help it capture its prey, such as small mammals, rodents, birds, and lizards.

A serval grows to be 1 1/2 feet in height and up to 5 feet long. It weighs about 20 to 40 pounds when fully grown. But it is its coloration that is most distinctive—particularly the colors of the young.

The short hair of a young serval is yellowish-brown on its sides and back—often with a pattern of black stripes and spots. These colors are so similar to the colors of the short grassland areas in which it lives that young servals, which can remain motionless for long periods of time, are very difficult to detect. This protective coloration allows the parents to go off hunting while the babies remain behind—carefully and cleverly camouflaged in a nest of grass. Potential predators often pass by without noticing the young ones at all.

Young animals of many species are particularly defenseless for the first few days or weeks after birth. Young servals have been able to survive this difficult time in their lives by taking advantage of a unique form of camouflage. By hiding from their enemies they increase their chances for survival in the wild.

Servals enjoy water and will often swim after frogs and fish in small pools or marshes.

The casque-headed frog is found primarily in the South American country of Ecuador. Other varieties of these frogs are located in the jungles of Southeast Asia and the rain forests of South America. They average about 2 to 3 inches long.

Hideous Hiders

One look at this creature and you might think you were observing an alien from another planet or some monster in a science-fiction movie. However, the strange appearance and unusual features of this animal help it survive from day to day.

The casque-headed frog is one of a group of several frogs whose shape, color, and appearance make them look exactly like dead and fallen leaves in the jungles where they live. Extra flaps and folds of skin jutting out in several directions, a pointed snout, brown and mottled skin,

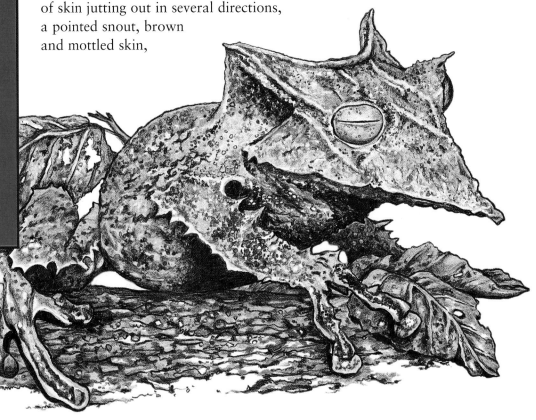

either making its home among the leaf litter that covers the forest floor or living up in the branches of rain forest trees. There it can rest or remain motionless for long periods of time—blending into the natural background.

The casque-headed frog also has another unique trait. After mating, the female frog carries all her eggs on her back for many days. There, the eggs hatch directly into young frogs. The tiny frogs stay "on board" their mother until they are old enough to venture out on their own.

and a bumpy body help this creature blend in with the plant life in which it lives.

As a result, this curious frog appears almost invisible among leaves on the ground.

Its camouflage helps the casque-headed frog in two ways. First, the frog easily escapes detection from any potential enemies. Snakes and other tropical predators like nothing better than a tasty frog for dinner, and this frog's camouflage helps it avoid becoming part of a snake's diet. Second, their camouflage also allows them to wait, without being seen, for their own food to arrive.

Like most frogs, the casque-headed frog is insectivorous (they primarily eat insects). Crickets, ants, or termites that get too close to this well disguised creature quickly become its next meal.

The casque-headed frog is primarily a terrestrial animal. That means that it spends its entire life on land rather than in the water—

All frogs must close their eyes in order to swallow. They use their eyeballs to help push food down their throats.

The orchid praying mantis inhabits the jungles of Southeast Asia. It is found mostly on the island nation of Malaysia. Its existence, however, is threatened due to the destruction and deforestation of large tracts of rain forest land in that tropical country.

Ferocious Flowers

If you were to go into your garden or the garden of a neighbor, you might see a wide variety of pretty flowers. Many of those flowers would have beautiful smells, and lovely blossoms. But if you were in Southeast Asia, you might want to think twice about bending down and smelling the blossoms of a wild rhododendron—particularly if you were a small (and tasty) insect.

The orchid praying mantis lives among the blossoms of the wild rhododendron bushes typically found in this tropical environment. Because of its color, shape, size, and special features this insect is almost impossible to distinguish from the bunches of flowers on this plant.

The mantis' forelimbs closely resemble parts of one of the flowers in a group of closely packed blossoms. Its body parts look exactly like a nearby blossom. And its hind legs closely match the parts of yet another flower in the bunch.

The orchid praying mantis is colored a delicate shell-pink all over—even its eyes and antennae are pink. As a result, it takes on the exact coloration of the flowers on which it rests. Unless you looked very closely (something insects don't often do) you would not even know this animal wasn't part of a flower.

All praying mantises eat their victims alive. And females sometimes eat their mates.

The orchid praying mantis is a **carnivorous** (meat eating) insect. When it is ready to eat, it waits patiently on the rhododendron flowers. Flying insects looking for nectar approach the flowers and are quickly seized with a lightning-quick movement by a pair of powerful pink claws. The long front legs of a mantis can close rapidly at the joints, snapping shut like a jackknife. These legs also are armed with several rows of teeth. Once a victim is caught by a praying mantis, it cannot escape.

This insect looks so much like a flower that it is able to stay in the same place for days and capture all the food it wants. Its dinner is always delivered by air— right to its table.

The sea dragon is a species of sea horse that lives in and around the coral reefs of Australia. Other sea horses live in shallow coastal areas throughout the world.

They range in size from the dwarf sea horse (1/2 inch long) to the Pacific sea horse (1 foot long).

Delicate Dragons

Living in the ocean can be very dangerous. Large fish and other marine creatures are always on the lookout for smaller organisms to turn into a tasty meal or a quick snack. Some sea animals can swim rapidly from their enemies. Others can dart in and out of rocks and plants. But one of the most unusual "hiders" in the sea may be the sea dragon, a species of sea horse that inhabits tropical oceans.

One of the most distinctive features of a sea horse is that it has a hard bony skeleton on the outside of its body as well as another skeleton on the inside. Its shape makes it look like a horse swimming through the water. Its scientific name— *Hippocampus*—means "horse-caterpillar."

The sea dragon has a long spiny body, bony head, and tubular snout. But it also has something else—lots of

A sea dragon moves
the fan-shaped fins on
its back at a speed of
2,100 beats per minute.

seaweed-like growths covering its entire body. It even has growths coming out of its nose, its head, and along the sides of its body. Unless you looked very carefully, you would think that it was just another piece of seaweed floating in the water.

Because the sea dragon looks so much like seaweed it is able to hide from enemies such as the sea turtle. It is able to curl its prehensile tail around a plant and remain perfectly still for long periods of time, swaying and moving with the plants so that it is barely recognizable.

Sea dragons travel by filling an internal swim bladder with air (so they rise in the water) or by emptying the bladder (so they sink). By changing the amount of air in their swim bladders, sea dragons can go up and down at will. To swim forward or backward, they use the fan shaped fins on the back and sides of their thin bodies. Even when sea dragons swim they are difficult to see, because they travel very slowly,

and only their transparent (see-through) fins move.

The sea dragon has eyes that work independently of each other. That means one eye can be looking downward while the other eye is looking upward. This is useful in locating food or any potential predators.

Leaping Lizards

If you were to walk through a tropical rain forest you might notice that the trees have lots of bumps and ridges. Many of these occur naturally on the bark of a tree, but some may not be related to the trees at all. In fact, they are often separate organisms such as plants or animals. One of the most unusual animals to make its home on the trunks of rain forest trees is probably one you would scarcely notice—that is, until it "flew" through the air to another tree.

This distinctive animal is the flying gecko, a creature whose coloration makes it look exactly like the bark of the trees on which it lives. The flying gecko's colors naturally blend in with the brown and black mottling (spotted coloring) of those trees. Even its skin has the patterns and indentations of tree bark.

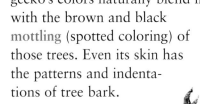

The flying gecko can remain motionless and unseen until a tasty insect comes too close and is quickly gobbled up. Geckos have very large eyes and well-developed hearing organs which assist them in locating their food, particularly at night when they are most active.

Although flying geckos are cleverly camouflaged against tree surfaces, they have also developed a distinctive way to elude (get away from) any would-be enemies. Besides a broad leaf-like tail, these creatures have wide flaps of skin along the sides of their bodies and narrow skin flaps along the

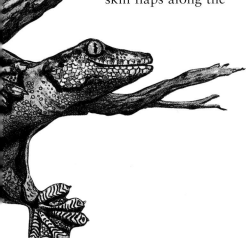

sides of their heads. When threatened, the flying gecko leaps into the air and spreads its legs out to the sides so that they act like the wings on a glider. By making its body flatter and wider it falls through the air like a parachute. In this way it can glide from tree to tree and easily escape.

Another interesting feature of this animal is its ability to cling to almost any surface. The flying gecko's feet have broad toes covered with ridges of scales. These scales have thousands of microscopic hooks that can hang onto almost any surface. As a result, the flying gecko can run over, under, and around its environment to chase after a meal or to escape another animal.

Its special feet even allow it to hang upside down from tree branches or smooth surfaces for long periods of time.

Geckos range in size from 1/2 inch to 14 inches. These remarkable creatures also have the ability to break off their tails when attacked. A new tail grows in its place in a few months.

A flying gecko is able to lick and clean its eyes with its tongue.

Stalking Sticks

STOP! FREEZE! Sit perfectly still! Don't move a muscle! How long do you think you can hold that position? If you're like most people, you find it very difficult to stay motionless for any great length of time. But there is an amazing creature that probably lives in your back yard or in a nearby forest that can remain motionless for many hours. Not only can it stay perfectly still, but its body shape makes it look exactly like the twig or branch on which it rests. As a result, this creature— the walking stick—is almost invisible.

Walking sticks are members of a family of insects with the scientific name *Phasmidae.* This is a Greek word which means apparition (ghost or phantom).

Walking sticks are extremely thin, with long spindly legs and compressed bodies. Depending on the species, they grow to be 2 1/2 to 4 inches long. Their antennae may be 1 3/4 to 2 1/2 inches long. Typically

Some species of walking sticks reproduce by parthenogenesis (the ability of a female to lay fertile eggs without mating). There is a species in New Zealand in which males have never been discovered!

they are green or brown so that they look exactly like a twig, stick, or plant stem. In fact, all their body parts resemble plant parts. When they walk, these curious creatures look like moving twigs. When they stand still, which they do quite often, they look like an extension of a branch or stick.

Many species of walking sticks can change their colors according to the season of the year. In spring or summer they are light to dark green, and can easily hide among the leaves of trees. In fall and winter they are able to change their colors to shades of brown and gray, concealing themselves among the branches of deciduous trees (those that lose their leaves in autumn).

The walking stick is quite common throughout the United States. Although it is hard to see in its natural environment, its eating habits can easily be detected. In fact, it is considered a pest in some sections of the country simply because it defoliates (eats the leaves from) large tracts of trees.

Although the walking stick is cleverly camouflaged in its natural environment, it is often located by predators such as birds, midges (small blood-sucking insects), and wasps. If captured, it has a unique trick to escape: It can break off one of its own legs—and leave the attacker with a very small body part to eat. The walking stick later grows a new leg.

Ptarmigans can be found in all the higher latitudes of the world including Scandinavia, Siberia, Alaska, northern Canada, Greenland, and Iceland.

Feathered Fashions

How would you like to be able to naturally change the color of your hair whenever you wanted? What if you could change your hair to blond or white in the winter, to black or brunette in the spring and summer, and to gray in the fall? That ability would be most unusual, especially if you could do it year after year. Well, you're about to meet an animal that does that—the ptarmigan.

The ptarmigan is a medium-sized bird that lives in some of the coldest regions of the Northern Hemisphere. This environment is often **barren**—having nothing more than large open expanses of rocks, short vegetation, and long rolling meadows. The climate in these regions is particularly harsh, with temperatures constantly below freezing. Snow and ice cover much of this land for most of the year.

Because of this open environment and lack of good hiding places, animals such as the ptarmigan are particularly susceptible to predatory animals such as

peregrine falcons and foxes. To survive, the ptarmigan has developed a unique camouflaging ability—it can change the color of its plumage (feathers) according to the season of the year.

In the winter, ptarmigans are almost completely white. The color of their plumage and ability to burrow into the snow makes them blend in perfectly with the rest of the landscape. In fact, it's even difficult to locate a whole group of ptarmigans walking across the snow.

In the spring and summer, the feathers of the ptarmigan change again. Males will have feathers that are gray or mottled brown in color, while females may have a variety of brown or black markings often touched with yellow. The colors blend with open patches of ground created by the melting snows.

During the autumn months, the ptarmigan's feathers become grayer in color, to help camouflage themselves among the rocks and dying plant life during this part of the year.

In addition to their changing colors, ptarmigans increase their chances of survival by crouching low on the ground at the first sign of a predator. By staying close to the ground their plumage blends in with the surrounding area. It is only when danger is very close that they fly away.

The whiteness of the ptarmigan's feathers in winter helps prevent too much heat loss from the bird's body.

Sargassum fish are named after the Sargasso Sea—a large expanse of water in the Atlantic Ocean filled with enormous beds of seaweed. This 3-inch fish can be found in many of the warmer areas of the Atlantic Ocean.

Swimming Seaweed

How would you like to be able to walk through a yard or across a park and be almost invisible? What if your body looked like it had branches, leaves, twigs, and other growths sprouting all over it—so many green and brown extensions that you looked just like a bush?

The sargassum fish looks so much like a piece of seaweed that it is almost impossible to locate when hiding. One look at this fish and you would think that it was a plant with fins. In fact, that's exactly how it is supposed to look! It lives in brown and gold colored seaweed—the same colors as the fish.

Another unique feature of this fish is its body. It is covered with a variety of flaps and extensions—that all look like pieces of floating seaweed.

Its skin, too, is covered with tattered flaps and spiky edges growing in all directions. Spiny **protrusions** (things that stick out) grow on its head and along its belly.

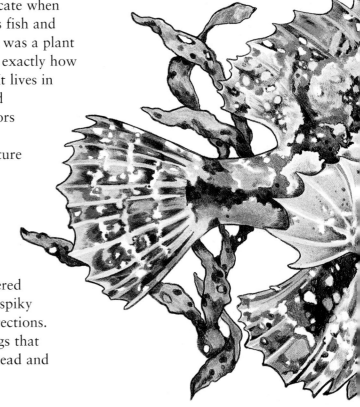

Its coloration and distinctive body parts conceal the sargassum fish in the sargassum weeds and other marine plants where it lives. There it remains, very still, hiding from its

enemies—usually larger fish that frequently visit seaweed beds. In this way it avoids becoming a meal for something else!

Its shape and color also help it hide while waiting for smaller fish to swim nearby. Since the sargassum fish has several yellow growths sticking out from its body, other fish think these look like pieces of food drifting through the water. Smaller fish swim up to nibble at the sargassum fish's growths and GULP—they quickly become a tasty meal!

Fantastic Fact

Although the sargassum fish is relatively small it can eat other fish nearly as large as itself.

There are approximately 50 different species of living stone plants—all of which inhabit the dry, arid regions of South Africa.

Pretty Pretenders

Animals aren't the only organisms that use camouflage to survive in the wild. There is a group of special plants—known as living stones—that also uses camouflage to their advantage.

As you might imagine, life in the desert can be harsh and severe. Both plants and animals need to have special ways of surviving in this sometimes desolate environment. Living stones

form a solid stone-like body. Their shape makes them look like rocks with small cracks etched across their tops. To complete their camouflage, the leaves are "sprinkled" with small dots or flecks that resemble small bits of minerals. As a result, these plants appear to be just another group of desert rocks.

When the rains come, each of these plants blossoms with a single tiny flower—usually yellow or white—that pokes up between the tightly bunched leaves. The flowers do not last for very long and pollination, usually by wind or insects, occurs very rapidly.

are also known as stone-plants, stonefaces or pebble plants. They are able to survive because they have characteristics of something they are not—a group of pebbles or small stones.

Rainfall is infrequent in the desert, and plants that live in these regions of the world must be able to germinate (sprout), grow, flower, and produce seeds very rapidly.

Usually less than 1 inch tall,

these ground-hugging plants have paired leaves that are joined beneath the ground to

Each leaf has a collection of very tiny "windows" that permit light to reach inside the plant.

Living stones have been able to adapt to a cruel and severe environment. Their size, shape, and color protect them from the long dry spells of the region as well as from desert animals looking for a quick meal.

The following are some of the groups throughout the country that are working hard to preserve and maintain the environment. Write or call them to find out what they are doing nationally, as well as how you can become involved in some of their local efforts.

Desert Protective Council
P.O. Box 4294
Palm Springs, CA 92263
(This group is working hard to preserve and protect the fragile desert environments of the U.S.)

Friends of the Earth
530 7th Street, SE
Washington, D.C. 20003
(Works to protect wildlife and wildlife habitats at the local, national, and international levels.)

The organisms in this book represent some of the most distinctive and unusual creatures on this planet. The ability of many animals and plants to camouflage themselves is how those organisms are able to survive in the places they live.

A group of living organisms of a single species living in a specific place is known as a population. Each population of animals shares some space with the populations of other animals. Clusters of animal populations living together are known as communities. All living things in a community are affected by all the other living things (as well as some non-living things such as water, soil, and rocks). The study of these relationships is called ecology.

For many animals, just living from day to day is a constant struggle. They must compete for food and they must avoid becoming a food source for other creatures, too. Often, that daily struggle for survival becomes complicated when humans enter the picture. When people build housing developments or pump dangerous toxins into the air with their cars or factories, then a nearby community of animals may be seriously affected. Some animals may not be able to hide because the plant life has been destroyed; other animals may not be able to find necessary food because the food has died as a result of being exposed to hazardous chemicals. The introduction of non-living things into an environment (for example, pollutants, highways, and buildings) has an effect on the survival and existence of all the living things in that environment.

Protecting and preserving wildlife and vegetation is an important concern around the world. What we put into an environment may have an impact on the survival of the many different communities that exist within that environment. In short, we affect how animals and plants are able to reproduce, grow, and live. That means that we must all work together to prevent or eliminate these environmentally harmful conditions.

Take some time to talk with your friends or classmates about ways in which humans affect the environment. Ask your school or local librarian for suggested books on environmental issues and problems.

Take a walk around your local neighborhood and note the various types of plants and animals that live there. What are some dangerous or harmful things in that environment that might affect the lives of those organisms? What can you and your friends do about those conditions? What you do now can have a positive affect on plants and animals in the years ahead.

Working with other people can make a difference in the survival of animal and plant populations. Find out as much as you can and share your knowledge with others. Your work is important to all living things.

Greenpeace
1436 U Street NW
Washington, D.C. 20009
(This organization deals with major issues affecting the oceans of the world. These issues may include whaling, pollution, and over-fishing.)

Izaak Walton League
1401 Wilson Boulevard
Level B
Arlington, VA 22209
(Concentrates on the cleanup and preservation of natural waterways such as streams and rivers.)

Nature Conservancy
1815 North Lynn Street
Arlington, VA 22209
(Purchases large pieces of land throughout the United States and around the world. This organization works to preserve those lands in their natural state.)

Sea Dragon

My Amazing Animal Adventures

The date of my adventure: _____

The people who came with me: _____

_____

Where I went: _____

What amazing animals I saw:

_____   _____

_____   _____

_____   _____

_____   _____

The date of my adventure: _____

The people who came with me: _____

_____

Where I went: _____

What amazing animals I saw:

_____   _____

_____   _____

_____   _____

_____   _____

SMART SURVIVORS

NATURE'S MOST AMAZING ANIMALS
Sneed B. Collard III

About Survivors

We've all got problems. We're behind in our homework. Our hair is too long or too short. Our sisters or brothers keep borrowing our clothes. Some days we have more problems than we know what to do with! But we have other problems that we usually don't even think about.

Each day we need enough water to drink and enough food to eat. We need to stay warm and breathe enough oxygen. We need a place to live, and we need to communicate with the people around us. If we did not solve each of these problems, we would soon perish.

In order to survive, animals and plants face many of the same problems. Different organisms solve these problems in an astounding variety of ways. Each method works for that species, but some plants and animals survive in ways that seem *especially* amazing or "smart."

In this book you'll meet some of the smartest survivors on our planet. You'll learn how they defend themselves, how they get enough food and water, and how they solve other problems. As you read, think about the problems each survivor faces, and think about how other animals and plants solve the same problems. You might be surprised to realize that each and every living thing—including you and me—is a smart survivor in its own special way.

DASHING DEFENDERS
Nudibranchs

GARY MILBURN/TOM STACK AND ASSOCIATES

When we think about survival, one of the first things likely to pop into our heads is finding enough food. But for most plants and animals, it's just as important to avoid *becoming* food. Some animals use claws or scales to avoid being eaten. Others hide from their enemies. Among the all-time self-defense champions, though, is a group of sea slugs called nudibranchs (NOOD-I-BRANKS).

Nudibranchs are closely related to snails and land slugs. Like land slugs, nudibranchs have no shells to protect them. Being shell-less could make nudibranchs easy targets for predators. But nudibranchs aren't as defenseless as they seem. Many species blend in with their surroundings, so predators have a hard time seeing them. Other nudibranchs display dazzling shades of orange, violet, red, and yellow as a warning to predators: "If you eat me, you'll be sorry!"

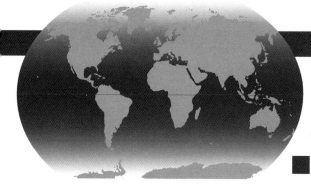

About 2,500 species of nudibranchs live in the world's oceans. Most are found in the warm waters of the tropics, but nudibranchs live in colder waters, too. Some nudibranchs are so small they fit between grains of sand. Others grow to over 12 inches. Most are about an inch long.

Where nudibranchs live

Predators pay attention to a nudibranch's colorful warning for good reasons. The skin of many nudibranchs is filled with acids and other chemicals that make the sea slugs taste bad. Other nudibranchs are armed with stinging cells called **nematocysts** (NEE-MAT-O-SISTS). Amazingly, the nudibranchs have to steal their stinging cells from other creatures.

Nudibranchs steal stingers from sea anemones, corals, and other animals they eat that are loaded with nematocysts. The stingers are like little poison darts that "fire" when they're touched by unwelcome visitors. Some kinds of nudibranchs, though, can swallow nematocysts without triggering them. Instead, the nudibranchs store the stinging cells in the feathery projections on their backs. When a predator tries to touch or bite one of these nudibranchs—OUCH!—the stingers fire, and the showy sea slugs go their own way.

WATER WIZARDS
Kangaroo Rats

A water wheel won't turn unless water is flowing through it. Life on the earth is the same way. Without water, all living things would grind to a halt. People and other mammals are especially dependent on water. To survive, an adult human must take in about two and a half quarts of water each day. Water is so important that most mammals can't survive in a dry desert. But kangaroo rats are able to do just that.

WENDY SHATTIL/BOB ROZINSKI/TOM STACK AND ASSOCIATES

Most mammals need a lot of water because they *lose* a lot of water. Mammals lose a lot of water simply by breathing. Before air enters a mammal's lungs, it must be warmed and moistened by special tissues in the animal's nose called **mucous membranes**. When a mammal breathes out again, it often loses all the water in that warm, moist air.

Kangaroo rats, though, have a "nose for water." When a kangaroo rat breathes out, the water in its breath collects like dew inside the rat's nostrils. In this way, the rat recycles the water, using it again and again.

Kangaroo rats are small rodents that inhabit open, arid places such as the Great Plains and the deserts of the Southwest. They live from southern Canada to Mexico. There are about 24 species of these hopping rodents and, not including their handsome tails, they're four to six-and-a-half inches long. They're named for their kangaroo-style hop, but don't be fooled: Kangaroo rats are not kangaroo kin.

Where kangaroo rats live

To save water, kangaroo rats also look beyond the ends of their noses. The animals have no sweat glands, so they don't lose water by perspiring through their skin. They also have special kidneys that use just one-fifth the amount of water human kidneys need to get rid of bodily wastes. And kangaroo rats spend their days in underground burrows, where they stay cool and moist even in scorching weather.

How do these desert rats get water in the first place? The answer is surprising: They eat seeds. The seeds look dry, but to the kangaroo rat they are instant water holes. As it eats, a kangaroo rat absorbs water from the seeds. Even more water is released when the seeds are broken down by the kangaroo rat's body. "Squeezing" seeds allows kangaroo rats to live in the driest deserts without drinking a drop.

LOVERS OF LIGHT
Strangler Figs

Plants are boring, right? Wrong! Plants—like animals—are often locked in deadly contests to get enough energy, nutrients, space, and water. In rain forests, so many plants and trees grow so close together that sunlight is in short supply. One group of plants called **epiphytes** (EP-I-FITES) gets around this problem by living in the tops of trees and in other plants. Many epiphytes do not harm the plants they live in, but strangler figs will kill for a little sunlight.

JOHN SHAW

KEVIN SCHAFER/MARTHA HILL/TOM STACK AND ASSOCIATES

Most trees start life in the ground, but not strangler figs. Their seeds sprout in the tops of other trees, where they're dropped by fig-eating birds, bats, and other animals. In the top of the tree, a strangler fig seed receives plenty of sunlight and starts growing. New branches and leaves climb toward the sky, while roots snake down the trunk of the fig's "host tree." The strangler's roots hold the young fig tree in place, and when the roots reach the ground, they start absorbing nutrients and water that the fig needs to grow.

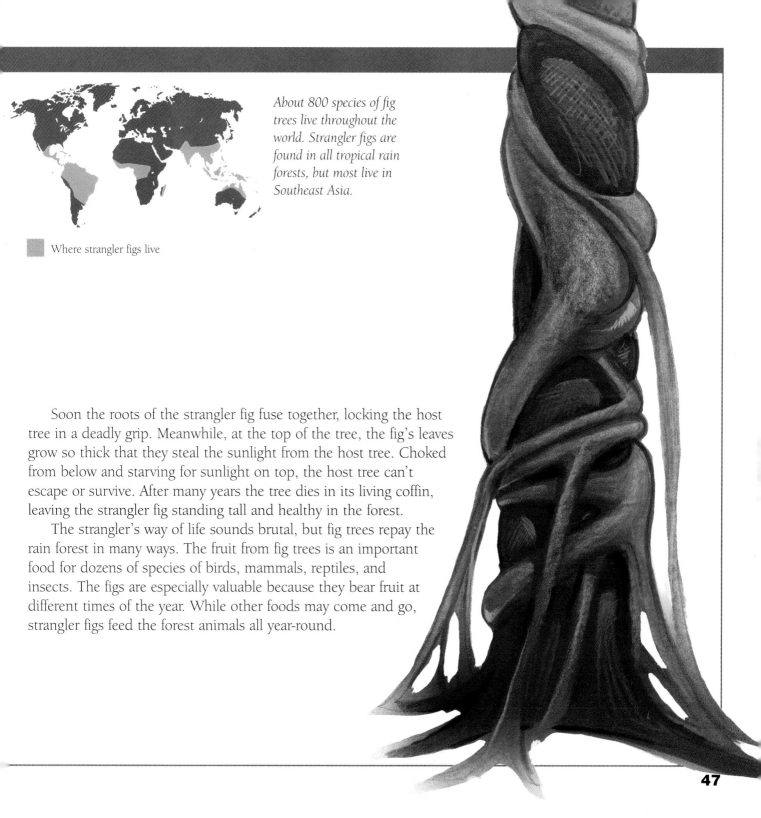

About 800 species of fig trees live throughout the world. Strangler figs are found in all tropical rain forests, but most live in Southeast Asia.

Where strangler figs live

Soon the roots of the strangler fig fuse together, locking the host tree in a deadly grip. Meanwhile, at the top of the tree, the fig's leaves grow so thick that they steal the sunlight from the host tree. Choked from below and starving for sunlight on top, the host tree can't escape or survive. After many years the tree dies in its living coffin, leaving the strangler fig standing tall and healthy in the forest.

The strangler's way of life sounds brutal, but fig trees repay the rain forest in many ways. The fruit from fig trees is an important food for dozens of species of birds, mammals, reptiles, and insects. The figs are especially valuable because they bear fruit at different times of the year. While other foods may come and go, strangler figs feed the forest animals all year-round.

TWILIGHT TALKERS
Fireflies

Communication is important to almost every animal. People communicate by talking, by writing, and even by stomping up and down. Other animals communicate in astonishing ways, but one way seems almost magical—the firefly's light.

Plants, animals, and other organisms that make their own light are called **bioluminescent** (BI-O-LOOM-I-NEH-SENT). Hundreds of organisms, from fungi and worms to fish and squid, are bioluminescent. Some organisms use light to attract prey. Others use it to blend in with their surroundings. However, the firefly is one of the few animals that uses light to "talk" to its own kind.

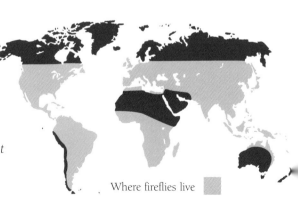

Fireflies aren't really flies. They're beetles. Fireflies live all over the world, including North America, but most live in the tropics. All together, there are about 2,000 species.

Where fireflies live

ROBERT AND LINDA MITCHELL

48

A firefly's light is produced by chemical reactions that take place inside the "light organ" on its abdomen. Fireflies use light mostly to attract mates, but different fireflies talk in different ways. In North America, the males of several species fly around while the females sit on the ground or on leaves. When a male firefly flashes, the female flashes back, which helps the male find her. If the female flashes too soon or waits too long, the male instinctively knows he is talking to the wrong species, so he stays away.

Flashes can be deceptive, though. The female of one kind of firefly sometimes imitates other firefly species. After she has mated with a male of her own species, she flashes at males of *other* species. The males land near her so they can mate. Instead of mating with these males, the female firefly eats them!

The most spectacular fireflies of all are the synchronous (SING-KRO-NUS) fireflies of Southeast Asia. Just after sunset, thousands of male synchronous fireflies start to flash, lighting up entire riverbanks in flashes of dazzling yellow. Scientists aren't sure why the fireflies flash at the same time, but that doesn't keep us from appreciating one of nature's most "illuminating" experiences.

ROBERT AND LINDA MITCHELL

ENERGY EXPERTS

Deep-Sea Vent Organisms

We are often taught that the energy for all life forms comes from the sun. The sun supplies energy so plants can grow. In turn, animals eat the plants—or they eat other animals that eat plants. But in 1977, a discovery at the bottom of the ocean changed our ideas about life on Earth. Scientists discovered a whole group of life forms that survive without any energy from the sun. These life forms are called deep-sea vent organisms.

Deep-sea vents are streams of hot water that bubble up from the ocean floor. They exist where large pieces of the earth's crust called **tectonic plates** are sliding together or spreading apart. Scientists found the deep-sea vents while they were exploring the ocean in submarines. When they discovered the vents, they were stunned. Hundreds of animals surrounded the vents—animals no one had ever seen before.

No one knew how these animals managed to survive, but it didn't take long to solve the riddle. The answer lay in a group of tiny organisms called bacteria. Bacteria live almost everywhere. Most eat other things or use the sun's energy to make their own food. But the deep-sea vent bacteria get energy by splitting chemicals called **sulfides**, which are found in the hot water that pours out of the vents. Later, the bacteria use this energy to make food for themselves.

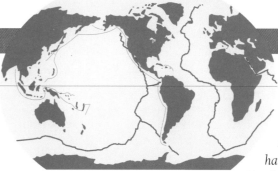

Deep-sea vents are found in areas where tectonic plates are sliding together or spreading apart. Vents have been discovered in the Pacific, Atlantic, and Indian oceans. Most deep-sea vents are no more than a few yards across, but in 1993, scientists discovered a vent field that covers 50 acres.

Anemones, mussels, shrimp, and limpets all feast on deep-sea bacteria. However, the most interesting vent animals are huge tubeworms called "vestimentiferans" (VEST-I-MEN-TI-FER-ENZ). These tubeworms grow over five feet high and form "worm gardens" around the deep-sea vents. The tubeworms have sulfide-splitting bacteria living inside their bodies. Both the worms and the bacteria benefit from this arrangement. The bacteria make food for the worms, while the worms give the bacteria a place to live.

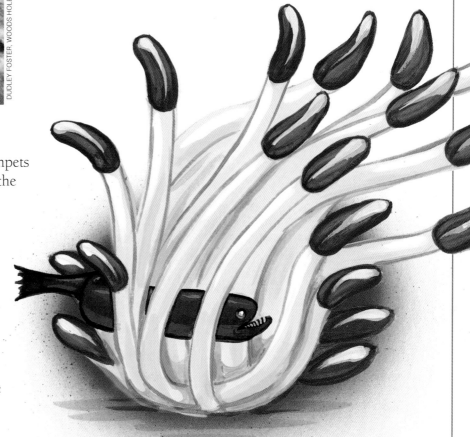

HEAT HOGGERS Polar Bears

Staying warm is a must for mammals. People stay warm by bundling up in coats and sweaters, or by staying indoors on cold days. But polar bears live outside in temperatures that reach 60 degrees below zero. How do they do it?

The first polar bears "hit the ice" between 100,000 and 200,000 years ago. Since then, the bears have evolved remarkable ways to stay warm in their freezing world. First of all, they have a thick layer of fat called blubber beneath their skin. Blubber insulates them from cold water, snow, and ice.

Polar bears live in one of Earth's harshest environments—the arctic. There, the bears prefer to live along the edges of the large ice sheets that cover the Arctic Ocean for much of the year. Polar bears also roam across the frozen arctic regions of Canada, Alaska, Greenland, the former Soviet Union, and other northern countries.

Where polar bears live

Polar bears eat mostly fat and meat—high-energy food that is converted into heat by the bears' bodies. To save energy, the bears sleep a lot, sometimes dozing off in the middle of a snow drift.

The most impressive thing that keeps a polar bear warm is its fur. A bear's fur is not really white—it's transparent. Each hair is like a tiny glass fiber that carries light from the sun to the bear. Beneath its "glass coat," the polar bear has black skin that absorbs heat very efficiently, keeping the animal warm.

A polar bear's fur converts 95 percent of the energy from light into heat—that's more than twice as efficient as any solar energy collector that people have invented. Scientists are studying polar bear fur so we can invent better ways to capture the sun's rays. Just by staying warm, polar bears may help us meet our future energy needs.

CLEVER CONSTRUCTORS
Weaver Ants

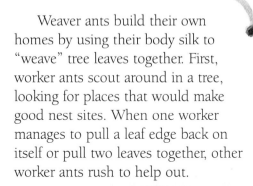

Everyone needs a place to live—even an ant. But finding a home is not always easy. Space on the ground may already be occupied. Cracks and crevices on plants and rocks may be in short supply. However, one group of ants weaves its way around this problem—the weaver ants.

ROBERT AND LINDA MITCHELL

Weaver ants build their own homes by using their body silk to "weave" tree leaves together. First, worker ants scout around in a tree, looking for places that would make good nest sites. When one worker manages to pull a leaf edge back on itself or pull two leaves together, other worker ants rush to help out.

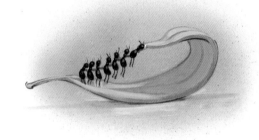

Several kinds of weaver ants build their own homes. The finest "ant architects"— those that build the most sophisticated shelters—live in the forested parts of tropical Africa, and from India to Australia and the Solomon Islands.

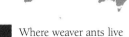

■ Where weaver ants live

Weaver ants live in colonies of up to half a million ants. A colony may inhabit more than 150 nests spread across several trees, but the ants use a nest only while its leaves are fresh. As soon as the leaves turn brown, they build a new nest. By building their own houses, weaver ants can survive in much larger numbers than insects that have to "find" houses.

By working together, ants pull the leaves into a shape that looks like a tent. Sometimes long chains of worker ants hold onto each other and pull leaves together.

When the leaves are in the right place, another group of worker ants carries weaver ant larvae out from nearby nests. The larvae make a silk or "glue" that dries quickly. By moving the larvae from place to place, the worker ants cement the leaves into a cozy nest about the size of a small coconut.

Weaver ants also protect the trees they live in by eating beetles and other animals that may damage trees. For over 1,700 years, Chinese people have used weaver ants to protect fruit trees from insect pests. Using ants to control pests is the earliest known example of **biological pest control** in human history.

NUTRIENT NABBERS
Cleaner Wrasses

People use weaver ants and other animals to control pests, but pest control in wild places often happens naturally. Many fish and other animals control pests simply by eating them. Among the flashiest of these nutrient nabbers are the "cleaner" wrasses.

MIKE SEVERNS/TOM STACK AND ASSOCIATES

Cleaner wrasses survive by picking dead tissue and **parasites** off of other fish. The parasites include fungi, bacteria, and small, shrimplike animals called **crustaceans** (KRUS-TAY-SHUNS). Parasites live on the skin, fins, and gills of all fish, and they can harm a fish by sucking its blood or eating its tissues.

To nab these parasites, cleaner wrasses set up "cleaning stations," usually next to a rock or a piece of coral. A cleaning station is like a car wash for fish. "Customers" are attracted by the wrasses' bright colors, and by a special swimming dance that the wrasses perform.

Wrasses live all over the world. One kind of wrasse called the giant wrasse grows over seven feet long, but most cleaner wrasses are shorter than a pencil. Cleaner wrasses are most often found in tropical waters.

Where cleaner wrasses live

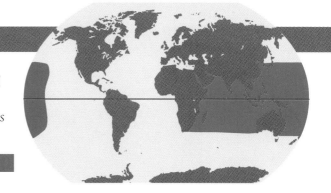

Fish that want to be cleaned hover next to the cleaning station, spreading out their fins and opening their mouths and gills. This kind of "posing" helps the wrasses find parasites and dead tissue.

Working alone or in pairs, cleaner wrasses swim all around their customer fish, picking parasites off with their sharp, tweezer-like teeth. The customers are usually much bigger than the wrasses. They could easily swallow the cleaners, but instead they wait patiently. Many fish even let the wrasses swim safely inside their gills and mouths.

Hundreds of fish species stay healthier by visiting cleaning stations. The cleaning service helps the wrasses, too. They could find food almost anywhere, but cleaning stations make life easier. For them, it's like having a "parasite pizza" delivered to their home every day of the week.

MARVELOUS MOVERS
Snakes

Kangaroos hop, birds fly, and people walk. Most of Earth's animals are on the move. Few methods of motion are more mysterious, spectacular, and startling than the sly slithering of snakes.

To get an idea of what it's like to be a snake, try sliding across a carpet on your belly, without using your arms or legs. For humans it's almost impossible, but for snakes it's a snap.

Snakes actually move in several ways. **Sidewinding** is the showiest. Sidewinding is used by snakes that move across sand or other shifting surfaces. A sidewinder keeps parts of its body pressed against the sand, while throwing or pulling the rest of its body forward. The name "sidewinding" comes from the fact that the snake's body is sideways to the direction that the snake is traveling.

Another popular snake movement is called **serpentine locomotion** (SUR-PEN-TEEN LO-KUH-MO-SHUN) because so many snakes, or "serpents," use it. In serpentine locomotion, a snake uses the sides of its body to push off of several different objects at once. These objects can be rocks, twigs, or even blades of grass. The snake's constant pushing allows it to move forward smoothly without using a lot of energy.

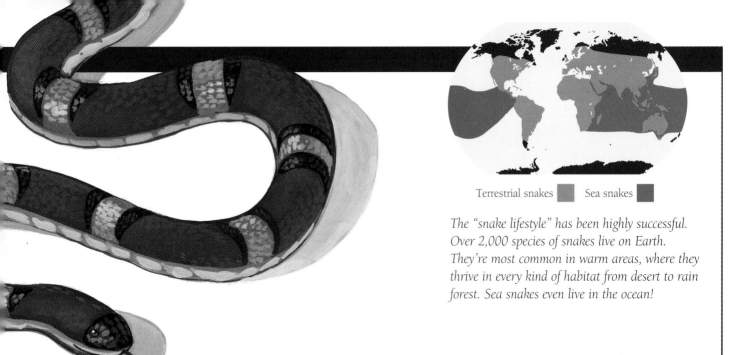

Terrestrial snakes [ ]   Sea snakes [ ]

*The "snake lifestyle" has been highly successful.
Over 2,000 species of snakes live on Earth.
They're most common in warm areas, where they
thrive in every kind of habitat from desert to rain
forest. Sea snakes even live in the ocean!*

A third snake motion is **rectilinear**
(REK-TI-LIN-E-AR) **movement**, which lets
snakes creep straight ahead without bending.
A snake accomplishes this by gripping the
ground with its "scutes" or belly scales, then
sliding its body forward inside of its skin.
Once the body has moved forward, the skin
"lets go" of the ground and catches up.

Snakes also jump, swim, ripple, and
glide through the air. Scientists have
discovered that when snakes move, they use
about the same amount of energy a lizard
uses to walk. But living without legs gives
snakes an advantage—it lets them slip
through holes and into tight places, where
they can find food and rest up for another
day of slithering.

C. ALLAN MORGAN

REMARKABLE REPRODUCERS
Bucket Orchids

If an organism doesn't reproduce, it won't survive. So the most important thing any organism can do is "make more of itself." When it comes to reproducing, few plants or animals are as clever as bucket orchids.

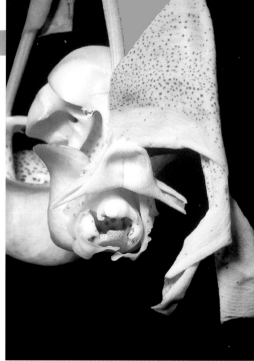

THE MARIE SELBY BOTANICAL GARDENS

THE MARIE SELBY BOTANICAL GARDENS

Like other flowers, orchids need to be pollinated or **fertilized** before they can make seeds. They depend on insects to carry pollen from one flower to another, and orchids use special tricks to attract the pollen carriers. Some orchids provide nectar for insects to eat. Other orchids lure insects with delicious smells. But the bucket orchid has its own bag of tricks.

The bucket orchid is named for the bucket-shaped trap that takes up most of its flower. Its "bucket" is about the size of a toy teacup, and it's filled with fluid. Like many other orchids, the bucket orchid attracts bees with a sweet-smelling, waxy substance.

About 35,000 orchid species inhabit the earth. Orchids are found in most parts of the world, but bucket orchids live only in the tropical forests of Central and South America. Like strangler figs, bucket orchids are epiphytes that cling to the tops of trees.

■ Where bucket orchids live

Bees land on the slippery rim of the bucket and try to scrape the sweet substance onto their legs. Before long, though, one of the bees slips into the bucket and sinks to the bottom.

The orchid does not drown its victim. The flower has a little "step" inside that leads to an escape tunnel. When the bee climbs into the tunnel—surprise! The tunnel slams down, gluing two little packets of pollen to the bee's back. The orchid flower pins the bee down for several minutes—long enough to ensure that the pollen is firmly in place. Then it releases the waterlogged insect.

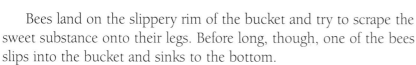

The orchid flower traps only the first bee that falls into its bucket. Other bees fall in, but they crawl through the escape tunnel without getting pinned inside. If the orchid is lucky, though, a bee carrying pollen from a *different* bucket orchid will pass through. When it does, the pollen on the bee's back is picked off by a little hook in the escape tunnel, and this pollen fertilizes the orchid. Then the bucket orchid "shuts its trap" and begins growing the seeds for a new generation of flowering tricksters.

PROTECTIVE PARENTS
Poison Arrow Frogs

Poison arrow frogs get their name from the highly toxic substances found in their skin. About 100 species of poison arrow frogs live in the tropical rain forests of South and Central America—moist, humid places that provide homes for water-loving amphibians like frogs, toads, and salamanders.

Reproduction is essential to animals as well as plants. It's especially important to make sure that young animals survive to become adults. Baby animals face many dangers—they might get eaten, get lost, die of thirst, or even starve to death. These risks are enough to drive poison arrow frog mothers right up a tree.

ART WOLFE

Poison arrow frogs don't take chances with their young. Parents hide their small batch of two to twenty eggs under damp leaves and guard the eggs until they hatch. In some species, Mom then gives her newly-hatched tadpoles a "piggyback ride."

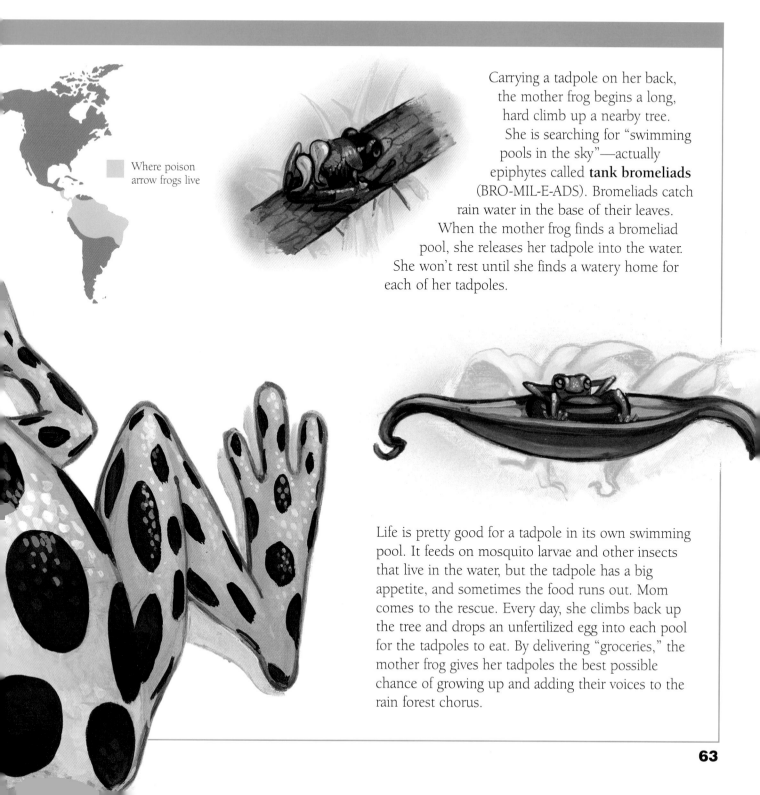

Carrying a tadpole on her back, the mother frog begins a long, hard climb up a nearby tree. She is searching for "swimming pools in the sky"—actually epiphytes called **tank bromeliads** (BRO-MIL-E-ADS). Bromeliads catch rain water in the base of their leaves. When the mother frog finds a bromeliad pool, she releases her tadpole into the water. She won't rest until she finds a watery home for each of her tadpoles.

Life is pretty good for a tadpole in its own swimming pool. It feeds on mosquito larvae and other insects that live in the water, but the tadpole has a big appetite, and sometimes the food runs out. Mom comes to the rescue. Every day, she climbs back up the tree and drops an unfertilized egg into each pool for the tadpoles to eat. By delivering "groceries," the mother frog gives her tadpoles the best possible chance of growing up and adding their voices to the rain forest chorus.

CHAMPIONS OF CHANGE
Human Beings

Sooner or later, one of nature's laws affects all living things: the law of change. Some organisms are good at adapting to change. Bacteria, for instance, constantly evolve into new forms that can survive in new ways or new places. However, among the world's larger animals, human beings are the "change champions."

LARRY MISHKAR

Human societies have coped with change for thousands of years. We have survived ice ages, droughts, volcanic eruptions, and countless other challenges. How have we done it? By using our special tools. One important tool is the human hand, which lets us pick up and move objects, plant crops, start warm fires, and build shelters. But an even more important tool is our **intelligence**.

Intelligence has given us the ability to figure out what's around us and how we can use our environment to survive. Our intelligence lets us respond to whatever happens, and even allows us to plan for what *will* happen in the future.

Where people *don't* live

People have colonized almost every habitat on our planet. We have learned to live in dry deserts, frigid polar regions, and steamy jungles.

LARRY MISHKAR

For millions of years, nature gave us changes we could handle with our intelligence. During cold times, people learned to wear clothes and find shelters so they could stay warm. During dry periods, people learned to store water or dig wells.

Over the last few thousand years, however, human activities have created even bigger changes. For example, by cutting down forests, we have raised the temperatures and lowered the amount of rainfall in some places. In other places, poor farming practices have caused soil to wash away, making it impossible to grow food on the land. Toxic chemicals made by people have poisoned streams, lakes, and oceans that once gave us healthy fish and clean water. All of these changes are more difficult to handle than the changes nature has thrown at us.

So far we've been able to use our intelligence in adapting to change. But as the human population gets larger and larger, our world is changing faster and faster. Will we survive? Probably. But what kind of world we live in depends on how well we plan for the future. If we hope to remain the champions of change, we'll have to use our smarts in new and better ways.

More About Smart Survivors

ERN MAINKA

There are thousands of "smart survivors" that we couldn't fit into this book. Scientists believe that between 10 and 30 *million* species of plants and animals live on our planet, and each species has its own ways of doing things. Scientists sometimes refer to the variety of different plants and animals on Earth as **biodiversity** (BIO-DI-VER-SI-TEE). The highest biodiversity probably exists in tropical rain forests and on coral reefs. Millions and millions of plants and animals make their homes in these places. But biodiversity is all around us. Hundreds of species of plants and animals—from birds to microscopic worms—live in our own back yards.

Yet each year, many species of plants and animals become extinct. People hunt some species to extinction, but most species disappear because people destroy their habitats.

The cutting and burning of rain forests, for example, has already destroyed thousands of species of insects and plants. Unless people stop this destruction, *millions* more may disappear.

Why is this a problem? First of all, each species of plant or animal is valuable just because it exists. Secondly, many of these plants and animals are useful to us. For instance, scientists have discovered a plant in Madagascar that helps control a disease called leukemia. Plants are also used to cure

DAVID HISER/PHOTOGRAPHERS/ASPEN

malaria and many other diseases. Finally, living with lots of different plants and animals makes our world more interesting and enjoyable. Imagine how boring Earth would be with only cows and grass to keep people company!

Preserving biodiversity is one of today's most urgent challenges. Governments, groups, and individuals are working hard to protect Earth's species.

U.S. Fish and Wildlife Service
Publications Unit
4401 North Fairfax Drive
Mail Stop 130 Webb
Arlington, VA 22203
(Works to protect endangered species, including polar bears)

Environmental Protection Agency
Public Information Center
401 M Street SW
Washington, D.C. 20460
(Concerned about biodiversity, endangered species, and many other issues)

The Nature Conservancy
1815 North Lynne Street
Arlington, VA 22209
(Protects predators, plants, and animals by safeguarding lands and waters)

Rainforest Action Network
450 Sansome Street
Suite 700
San Francisco, CA 94111
(Protects rain forests and rain forest peoples)

The National Wildlife Federation
1400 Sixteenth Street NW
Washington, D.C. 20036-2266
(Works on biodiversity, endangered species, and other important issues)

My Amazing Animal Adventures

The date of my adventure: _____

The people who came with me: _____

_____

Where I went: _____

What amazing animals I saw:

_____   _____

_____   _____

_____   _____

_____   _____

The date of my adventure: _____

The people who came with me: _____

_____

Where I went: _____

What amazing animals I saw:

_____   _____

_____   _____

_____   _____

_____   _____

SURPRISING SWIMMERS

NATURE'S **MOST AMAZING** ANIMALS

Anthony D. Fredericks

About Swimmers

Sea Otter

Have you ever been to a pool, a lake, or the ocean to go swimming? Swimming is one of the most enjoyable activities we do. We swim to cool off during a hot day, we swim for exercise and relaxation, and we swim to get from one place to another (to cross a lake, for example). Everybody, young or old, enjoys swimming.

Sea Snake

Many animals swim, too. Fish swim, birds swim, reptiles and amphibians swim, and mammals and insects swim. Animals swim for different reasons. For example, for dolphins, swimming is their primary form of locomotion, or travel. Ducks swim to locate food. For frogs, swimming is a way to escape from enemies. Salmon have to swim in order to mate. And, like you, some animals (including bears) swim for relaxation.

As you know, there are many ways to swim. Animals may swim on top of the water or under the water. Some animals swim 24 hours a day. Some swim in unusual ways. Still others are clumsy in their attempts to swim—have you ever seen a dog paddle? Some animals are natural swimmers; for others, it does not come so easily. There are, however, several animals whose swimming ability is nothing less than amazing!

In this book, you will have a chance to meet some of the most unusual swimmers in the animal kingdom. You will read about a lizard, a bird, and a spider, each of which can swim underwater. You will also learn about a snail and a snake, both of which can swim on top of the water. And you'll read about an insect that can swim backward! As you read, think about why a particular animal swims as it does and how its swimming ability helps it survive in the wild. You're sure to discover some fascinating facts about these 12 surprising swimmers of the animal world.

SQUIDS

Rocket Racers

Squids live in a variety of habitats throughout the world's oceans—from the warm waters of the tropics to the colder regions of the Atlantic and Pacific. In some countries, squid is prized as a food delicacy. As a result, squids have become endangered animals in some parts of the world.

The fastest a human being can swim is about 5 mph. If you were in a car going 5 mph you would think you were traveling quite slowly. But there's an animal that can swim six times faster than a human—up to 30 mph—and it's able to do it backward! This jet-propelled creature is the squid.

Size for size, a squid can outswim almost every other marine animal. It's able to do this because its rocket-shaped body is well suited for racing at high speeds. The squid's streamlined body also has powerful muscles that contract to force out a jet of water just like a blast from a fire hose.

These blasts occur repeatedly, allowing the squid to zig and zag through the water looking for food.

Like its cousin the octopus, a squid has eight arms covered with powerful suckers. In addition, it also has two tentacles (arms) that are used to capture small fish, crabs, and other sea creatures. When a fish is caught, the squid kills it with a bite from its mighty beak. It then removes the head of the fish and strips the flesh from its bones.

Squids are also noted for their excellent eyesight, which is more advanced than that of any other invertebrate (it has no backbone) in the animal kingdom. Not only does their eyesight help them locate food, but it also helps squids identify approaching enemies. When an enemy is sighted, squids protect themselves by emitting an inky fluid, and then dart from their pursuer into the cloudy water. As additional protection, squids can also change their colors, especially when excited.

A rocket-powered sea creature! An animal that can change its color whenever it wants to! Excellent eyesight and strong muscles! The squid must be a very intelligent creature because, like you, it is frequently found in schools.

Fantastic Fact

The famous giant squid of the Atlantic Ocean reaches a length of 50 feet and a weight of 2 tons. Its eyes are the size of basketballs!

The fire squid of the Indian Ocean has organs that flash light in different colors— blue, green, white, and red.

Slithering Sea Serpents

Sea snakes can be found from the Persian Gulf to Japan and south to Australia. They live in coral reefs, river mouths, mangrove swamps, and the open ocean. Like their land relatives, they come in a variety of colors. The most common are bright yellow with black markings.

Life in the ocean is sometimes difficult. Animals must be able to get their own food without becoming food for someone else. Many marine creatures have learned how to adapt to this frequently harsh environment by developing special skills or body parts that allow them to grow, develop, and reproduce for many generations. Certainly one of the most distinctive animals of this aquatic ecosystem is the sea snake.

Just like its cousins on land, the sea snake has developed specific features that help it survive. These creatures spend their entire lives in the ocean. As a result, their bodies are flattened side to side—a feature that allows them to travel through the water with ease. Their tails, shaped like the oars on a rowboat, also contribute to their swimming prowess.

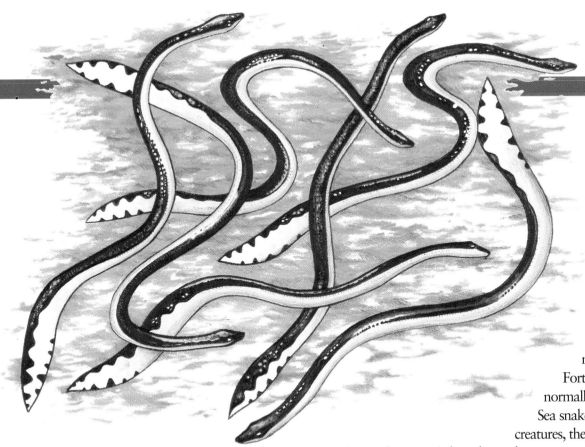

(have poison). They use their piercing fangs to inject poison directly into their victims, killing them in just a few moments.

Fortunately, they do not normally attack humans.

Sea snakes are communal creatures, they typically travel in large groups. Large schools of sea snakes are often found far out to sea, writhing and wiggling on the surface of the ocean in great numbers.

There are about fifty varieties of sea snakes—ranging in length from 3 to 8 feet—throughout the world. While most spend their entire lives swimming through the ocean, a few species come on land to lay eggs. Ocean-dwelling sea snakes, however, give birth right in the water.

Fantastic Fact

The largest group of sea snakes was spotted in the Malacca Strait in the South Pacific. This concentration of snakes was nearly 60 miles long.

Sea snakes are air-breathing animals and have developed a specialized lung, one that is considerably larger than the two lungs of their land-locked relatives. If necessary, this single lung allows sea snakes to stay underwater for up to 3 1/2 hours and dive to depths of 100 feet or more. This feature is important in helping sea snakes locate their primary food—eels and small fish.

Although few land snakes are deadly, all sea snakes are venomous

MARINE IGUANAS

Marine iguanas can be found only on the Galapagos Islands. Mostly black or gray in color with splotches of red, an iguana can grow to 4 feet in length. It is distinguished by a blunt snout, a flat tail used for swimming, and a very clumsy-looking body.

Diving Dragons

When you want to eat, you go to the grocery store, a fast food restaurant, or you open the refrigerator at home. You're able to eat many different kinds of food and are able to find that food in many different places. But, unlike you, the marine iguana eats only one type of food and must swim underwater to find it.

The marine iguana is a remarkable creature simply because it can be found entirely on one group of islands—the Galapagos Islands. This small collection of isolated islands is located 600 miles off the western coast of Ecuador, South America, in the Pacific Ocean. It is home to some of the most unusual plant and animal species in the world. One of those species, the marine iguana, feeds entirely on the algae

that grow on underwater rocks. Because it has partially webbed feet, the marine iguana can easily swim beneath the waves. It also has strong claws that help it hold on to the slippery rocks as it feeds. Occasionally, iguanas will swim out to feed beyond the surf, where their chief enemy, the shark, may catch an unsuspecting diner.

When they dive, iguanas can go as deep as 35 feet below the surface, although most will search for food on rocks 15 to 20 feet deep. Although they can stay underwater a long time, most iguanas will remain submerged (underwater) for about 15 to 20 minutes while feeding. Interestingly, the

Female marine iguanas dig tunnels as deep as two feet under the sand to lay their eggs.

This can be dangerous for the iguana—the tunnels could collapse at any moment.

marine iguana is the only lizard that uses the sea as its only source of food.

When they're not eating, marine iguanas will gather in tight bunches on the rocky shore, often piling on top of one another. Here, they bask in the sun, raising their body temperatures to between 95 and 99 degrees F before diving in the cool ocean waters to search for food.

While they sun themselves, small red crabs frequently crawl over and around the iguanas. These crabs use their pinchers to remove small blood-sucking ticks from the iguana's skin. The ticks are an important part of the crabs' diet.

Although a marine iguana looks fearsome, it is a mild-mannered creature. Occasionally, however, males will engage in short territorial fights in which they butt their heads together. Sometimes males will push each other around with their heads until one gives up and retreats.

Most of the time, however, they would rather sun themselves on the rocks or look for an underwater snack.

When scared, a marine iguana will blow salt water vapor from special glands in its nose—making it look just like a miniature dragon.

Backswimmers can be located throughout the world wherever there is standing water, in ponds, lakes, and canals. Its shape—with a ridge along its back and its characteristic "oars"—make it look like a slightly submerged rowboat.

Rapid Rowers

When you want to travel somewhere, usually you get on a bicycle or ride in a car. Normally you sit or stand right side up and move in a forward direction. For a moment, however, think how it would feel if you had to travel upside down and backward. There's an amazing animal that does just that—and doesn't mind one bit!

The backswimmer is a small insect—about 1/2 inch in length—that lives in ponds and lakes around the world. Pale brown in color, the backswimmer is

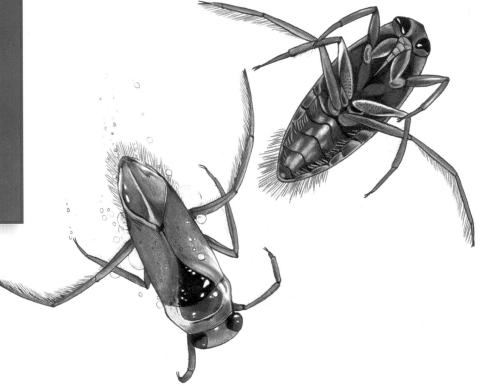

In winter when a pond freezes, backswimmers walk around upside down under the ice.

distinguished by long back legs fringed with fine hairs. These legs look just like a pair of oars on a rowboat.

For much of the day a backswimmer rests upside down just below the surface of the water. It is able to do this by capturing a small bubble of air at the surface and pressing it to its abdomen with a series of small bristles. Since it is also an air-breathing animal it has breathing holes called spiracles along the sides of its abdomen. It presses the captured bubble against those holes and obtains the oxygen it needs. If the backswimmer is frightened or threatened by an enemy, it may dive under the water carrying its bubble with it.

The backswimmer also swims on top of the water. This may be its most distinctive feature. Still upside down, the backswimmer uses its hind legs as oars and quickly propels itself across the surface of the water—away from any enemy.

It also uses this form of locomotion to attack and eat mosquitoes, tadpoles, and small fish. The prey is located by vibrations on the water. Scooting across the water, the backswimmer captures its meal, plunges its beak into the victim, pumps in some digestive juices, and then sucks out the animal's fluids.

Although the backswimmer prefers to swim backward, it also can fly. It flies, however, right side up and forward. A creature that can swim backward and fly forward is an example of the amazing diversity of organisms in the animal kingdom.

KRILL

There are about 85 species of krill, almost all of which inhabit the frigid waters off Antarctica. Krill feed on the billions and billions of tons of plankton that live in the icy waters of this region.

Frozen Food

How many hamburgers or hot dogs can you eat at one time? Two? Four? Ten? Like most people, your limit is probably two or three at a single sitting (you know what happens when you eat too many). Yet, in the Antarctic Ocean, whales will eat millions of a tiny sea creature—all in one gulp! It's not the whales that are distinctive, but the animals they eat—krill.

Krill are small, shrimp-like creatures that live in some of the coldest waters on the planet. A pair of eyes, long antennae, and eight pairs of branched legs

on its 2-inch body make it look like an alien being from a distant world.

What is so amazing about krill is their enormous numbers. **Shoals** (large groups) of krill commonly swim together through the icy waters of Antarctica. These groups may be as small as a few feet across to more than an acre—a whirling mass of billions and billions of organisms. These shoals may extend for hundreds of yards in circular, oval, or oblong shapes.

Although krill are the main food source of Antarctic whales, they are also a favorite of seals, penguins, sea birds, and other fish.

In fact, many scientists believe that krill are the most important link in the Antarctic food chain— their sheer numbers make them the most valuable food source for a wide variety of animals. Without that food source, there would not be sufficient nourishment for large numbers of polar animals.

Krill are **luminescent**—their bodies are composed of several light-producing organs. At night they light up and become an enormous mass of blue-green. During the day, however, they maintain their reddish color, looking like a gigantic pulsing plant beneath the surface.

Krill are an important food source for the animal populations of the Antarctic and are being considered as a potential food for humans, too. Because krill are high in protein, low in fat, and are readily abundant, several nations are developing plans to harvest these little creatures.

This could be dangerous in that some species of whales subsist almost entirely on krill and therefore may lose an important food source. To feed humans, we may be removing an essential and necessary food from the "table" of other animals, putting them at risk of elimination.

Harmful Hitchikers

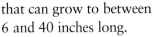

There are about 30 species of lampreys found in the temperate regions of the northern and southern hemispheres. Some live in salt water, others in fresh water. All lampreys, however, begin their lives in fresh water. As they grow, some move down rivers and into the ocean.

When people travel they may drive, ride, or fly. After they arrive at their destination they usually don't destroy their car, bicycle, or airplane. However, there is an animal that does just that—one that "catches" a ride with another animal, and slowly kills its host as they travel together. This hitchhiker, the lamprey, is a most unfriendly swimmer.

One look at a lamprey and you're likely to say that it's one of the ugliest creatures you've ever seen. A lamprey looks like an eel with a slimy scaleless body that can grow to between 6 and 40 inches long.

Its body has no bones whatsoever. In fact, a lamprey's

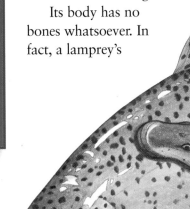

entire body is made of cartilage—the same rubbery material that shapes your nose. Most importantly, a lamprey does not have a jaw. Its head ends in a large funnel-like mouth. It is this mouth that makes the lamprey a very dangerous animal.

The lamprey's circular mouth is filled with dozens of pointed teeth. There are even teeth scattered across its muscular tongue. To feed, the lamprey searches for fish in lakes or rivers. When it locates one, it attaches itself to the side of the fish with its suction-like mouth. It then begins to scrape the fish's skin with its tongue and teeth. The fish begins to bleed, and the lamprey sucks up the blood.

The lamprey may remain attached for weeks or even months, traveling on its host wherever it goes and enjoying a free meal at the same time.

Eventually, the lamprey obtains all the food it needs and detaches itself from its host. At other times, lampreys may continue traveling and feeding until the host is killed.

In some parts of the world—the Great Lakes region of the United States, for example—lampreys have become a serious ecological problem. They multiply rapidly, attach themselves to large numbers of fish, and kill off entire populations of aquatic life. In recent years, a special poison has been developed to control this traveling pest.

Lampreys spend much of their lives swimming as an "attachment" to a fish. While they are capable of swimming on their own, they prefer to hitch a ride on an unsuspecting host. Unfortunately, this turns out to be a "death trip" for the helpful fish.

Fantastic Fact

The ancestors of lampreys have been traced back for 400 to 450 million years.

The sucker mouth of the lamprey is so strong it can pull itself up over rocks or vertical walls.

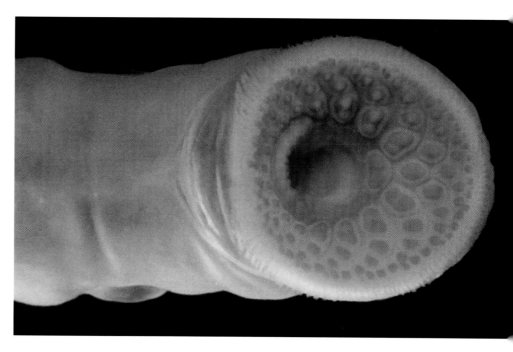

SCALLOPS

There are approximately 300 species of scallops living around the world. Since they prefer shallow water, their shells are often washed up on shore, particularly after severe ocean storms.

Speeding Shells

Lots of people enjoy eating seafood. Many people order lobster, crab, and other kinds of fish when they go out to eat. One of the most popular seafoods is the scallop, a shellfish common along the Atlantic Coast. Interestingly enough, scallops are rapid swimmers. Those you find on your plate in a restaurant, however, weren't fast enough!

Scallops are part of a group of animals called **bivalves**—animals with two shells. Varying in size from 1 to 8 inches, the 300 species of scallops can be

found throughout the world, typically living in shallow waters. Their shells, covered with ridges and corrugations, are pink, red, or yellow. The wavy edges of the shell are where we get the term "scalloped," which also describes a specific way some fabrics are cut.

Scallops lie on the sea bed with their shells open. Frequently, however, they zip through the water just like small jet-propelled submarines. To do this, a scallop opens its shell and fills the interior space with water. The powerful muscle inside quickly contracts, pulling the valves shut and shooting water out from behind. The scallop speeds forward through the water.

A scallop can lose all of its eyes and re-grow them in two months.

Depending on which way a scallop wants to go, it can dart forward or backward. Its motion, however, is erratic and side to side—resembling a saucer sinking in a container of water. Nevertheless, its jets of water are so strong it can blow away an approaching (and hungry) crab.

One of the most distinguishing features of this animal is its rows of tiny eyes along the edge of its mantle (fleshy skin that lines the inside of the shell). Depending on the species, scallops have between 30 and 100 well-developed eyes.

Most bivalves have two muscles, but the scallop has only one. It is this single muscle that is consumed by people around the world. Although the scallop is a quick swimmer and is able to dart away from its primary enemies—the starfish and octopus—it may not be quick enough to escape the chef at your favorite seafood restaurant.

GUILLEMOTS

Guillemots are birds of the north. Principally located in and around the North Sea, they can be found as far south as Portugal and North Korea. In many ways they resemble a duck, growing to 16 inches in length and sporting dark brown feathers and a white belly. Their numbers have decreased in recent years due to polluted oceans and an increasing number of oil spills.

Bathing Birds

Most birds live on land or up in trees. There they make their nests, raise their young, and search for food to feed themselves. When we think of birds, we think of creatures with wings that can fly through the air, traveling from place to place. Soaring, swooping, and diving, these magnificent creatures can be found on every continent in the world and in almost every back yard. But have you ever

seen a bird that flies underwater? The guillemot is a penguin-like bird which is able to do just that!

When it's not feeding, the guillemot lives near the water, building its nests on narrow ledges of towering cliffs. The nests of a guillemot colony, often hundreds of birds, are jammed so close together they are almost on top of one another.

Because they live by the sea, guillemots feed on many types of marine creatures including fish, sand eels, shrimp, crabs, mollusks, and worms. Since fish make up a major portion of their diet, they have developed a distinctive way of catching their dinner. Floating on the water, guillemots will kick their feet, partially spread their wings, and dip their heads.

This action pushes the birds underwater, where they use their

Fantastic Fact

Unlike most other birds, guillemots survive in extremely cold weather. The temperature can drop well below zero and most guillemots do not have to migrate to warmer climates.

wings for propulsion (pushing them forward) and their feet for steering. Here, the birds swoop, glide, and "fly" through the water just as they do in the air. The birds are so fast that fish are usually captured in the birds' beaks after short underwater chases.

Guillemots can travel almost as fast underwater as they can in the air. You can imagine how surprised fish might be when they see a whole flock of these birds swooping after them underwater.

Although guillemots spend a lot of time underwater, they can be found bobbing on top of the waves, too. Here, they rest between dives.

Like many other water birds, guillemots have waterproof feathers that are coated with a special oil to help keep them dry. The feathers are shed once each year and new ones are grown. As the new feathers are growing, guillemots are unable to fly or swim and must feed close to shore to obtain the food they need. The feathers grow fast, however, and soon the guillemots are able to soar over the waves and "fly" under the sea.

Gentle Giants

Beautiful in "flight," these graceful swimmers can be found in tropical and subtropical oceans around the world. Many large aquariums and oceanariums throughout the United States have devil fish on display, too.

Have you ever seen an eagle or hawk lazily gliding through the skies on currents of air? It seems to float on the wind, slowly winging its way across the sky. It can glide with the greatest of ease, occasionally flapping its wings or hovering over the trees.

There's an amazing creature that seems to glide through the water, swooping and soaring through the ocean. It's the devil fish—a relative of sharks, rays, and skates.

The devil fish has a flattened body with large triangular fins that look exactly like wings. A large mouth framed by enormous "horns" makes this creature look terrifying

and menacing. Sailors used to think this animal was one of the most dangerous in the ocean, hence its name. It is, however, only dangerous to small fish, crustaceans, and plankton, which it scoops into its mouth as it swims.

Devil fish are also known as **mantas**—the Spanish word for "blanket"—which refers to their widespread shape and size. Manta rays, the largest of the devil fish, measure up to 22 feet across. The smallest member of this group is the Australian pygmy ray which reaches a width of only 2 feet across.

Devil fish spend most of their time swimming in small groups of two or three, although they sometimes congregate in schools. Typically, they swim near the surface of the water with slow flapping motions of their gigantic pectoral fins. They often resemble enormous birds gracefully "flying" through the sea. Some people think they even look like colossal bats. As a result, they are sometimes referred to as "batfish."

Fantastic Fact

The largest recorded devil fish measured 60 feet across and weighed 5,000 pounds.

One of the most unusual "tricks" of these immense creatures is to leap high into the air, falling back to the ocean with a loud "whap!"—just like the sound you make when you do a "belly flop" off a diving board. The sound of these animals hitting the water can be heard for miles across a calm sea. No one is quite sure why they display this unusual behavior. It just adds to our appreciation and awe of these magnificent "eagles of the ocean."

Slimy Sailors

Have you ever floated on a raft at the beach, swimming pool, or lake? It's quite relaxing to lie on that cushion of air and pass the day away. How would you like to do it for your entire life? In fact, how would you like to float *upside down under a raft* for your whole life? The purple sea snail is one of the few

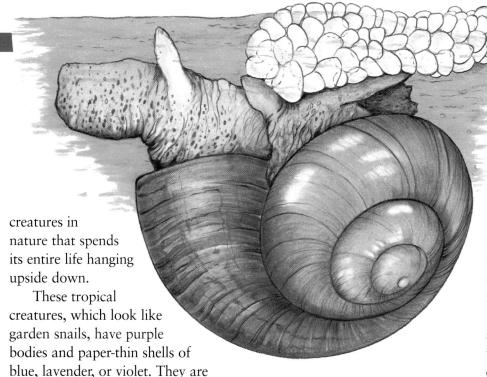

creatures in nature that spends its entire life hanging upside down.

These tropical creatures, which look like garden snails, have purple bodies and paper-thin shells of blue, lavender, or violet. They are seldom more than 2 inches in length and can be found in large numbers in the warm waters of the Atlantic, Pacific, and Indian oceans.

The purple sea snail hangs upside down by creating a small bubble raft. It secretes (oozes) froth from its foot, which traps air into a collection of bubbles. The bubbles are coated with a special mucus (slime) that hardens into a jelly-like substance. The snail glues all the bubbles together into a raft-like structure from which it hangs upside down. The snail spends its life floating along on ocean currents or carried around by ocean winds.

At first glance, you may think this little creature is quite harmless, but don't tell that to a jellyfish! Purple sea snails love to eat jellyfish. While they are floating, the snails can detect the presence of nearby jellyfish through special sense organs located near their mouths. Although sea snails have no eyes, they are quite good at finding their favorite food.

After a jellyfish is located, the sea snail releases a purple dye that anesthetizes (stuns) the jellyfish. Temporarily immobilized, the jellyfish's tentacles (with their stinging cells) are eaten by the snail until only the gas-filled float of the jellyfish remains. After feeding, the sea snail lays as many as 3 million eggs on the underside of the dead jellyfish.

Sometimes it is difficult for the sea snail to locate enough jellyfish to eat. During those times, these creatures become cannibalistic— eating members of their own colony in order to survive.

All purple sea snails are born as males. As they grow, they all become females.

PUFFER FISH

Puffer fish can be found in many of the tropical seas of the world, typically living in and among coral reefs. Here, they eat barnacles, sea snails, crabs, and worms. If taken out of the water, they fill their bellies with air instead of water.

Balloon Bodies

Stand in front of a full-length mirror and look at yourself. Now, inflate your lungs with as much air as you can and observe yourself once more. You'll probably notice little difference between your "deflated" body and your "inflated" body. But how do you think you would look if you could take in enough air to blow yourself up to twice your normal size?

Puffer fish, sometimes known as balloon fish, globe fish, blow fish, or swell fish, inflate their bodies to twice their normal size by taking in large quantities of water. They do this as a form of protection. Puffer fish have a very small gill capacity. They swim slowly and use little energy while swimming.

When threatened, these fish fill up their bellies with water (an 8-inch fish may take in as much as one quart of water), holding the water until the danger passes. By enlarging themselves with water and doubling their size, they appear to be much larger (and meaner) than they really are—thus fooling any would-be predators.

Although most predators would leave a larger prey alone, these clever creatures have another added defense—poison. Puffers are some of the most poisonous of all marine animals. They carry tetraodontoxin, a powerful nerve poison that causes a violent and rapid death when ingested. This poison is carried in the puffer's liver, reproductive organs, and intestines.

One of the most widely known of all puffer fish is the porcupine fish. When this fish—normally 1 to 2 feet in length—blows itself up, dozens of sharp spines stand out from its body. Each spine is about 2 inches long. These spines serve as protection from the fish's enemies.

Occasionally, however, an unsuspecting (or very hungry) shark will eat one of these fish. The porcupine fish may then inflate itself inside the shark's mouth where it remains stuck for some time—severely injuring the shark. If the shark survives this encounter, it will have learned a very valuable lesson.

Fantastic Fact

In Japan, puffer fish (known as *fugu*) are eaten as a delicacy. Specially trained cooks remove the poisonous parts before the fish are served. Still, every year, dozens of people die from eating this fish.

Furry Floaters

Sea otters were once almost hunted to near extinction for their fur. Once ranging along the entire Pacific Coast from Mexico up and around to Japan, their numbers are significantly lower today. Although laws are in place to protect them, those laws must be enforced to ensure the survival of this valuable species.

Have your parents ever told you not to play with your food? Well, you're about to meet an animal that not only plays with its food, but does so while it's swimming on its back.

The sea otter is a marine mammal that seldom comes on shore. It spends most of its time in small herds off the rocky shores of California, Alaska, and several northern Japanese islands. Long ago, there were many more sea otters than there are today. That's because the fur of the sea otter was highly prized. Fur hunters killed off millions of these animals before tough laws were passed in 1910 and 1911 to protect this valuable creature from extinction.

The fur of a sea otter is dense, thick, and glossy. It ranges in color from dark brown to black. A sea otter's head, throat, and chest are white.

Most interesting is how a sea otter's fur keeps it warm. Sea otters differ from other marine animals in that they have no fat or blubber under their skin to protect them. Air is trapped in their fur, acting as a protective barrier or insulation from the cold water. If the fur becomes covered with oil or other pollutants, it loses its insulating properties and the sea otter dies from **exposure** (it has no protection from cold water).

A sea otter spends most of its day floating on its back in offshore kelp beds. While it's resting or sleeping, it wraps strands of kelp around itself so it doesn't drift away. Every so often it will dive beneath the water—often to depths of 100 feet—to capture crabs, mussels, clams, abalones, and sea urchins for food. It will also grab a small rock or flat stone in its short paws.

When it returns to the surface, the sea otter floats on its back, uses its chest as a table, and uses the stone to crack open shellfish it has gathered from the ocean floor. In fact, the only time the sea otter doesn't float on its back is when swimming away from danger or diving for food.

Fantastic Fact

To survive, most sea otters need to eat about 20 pounds of food a day (that's one-fourth of their total body weight).

PROTECTING SURPRISING SWIMMERS

There are several organizations working to help preserve animal habitats around the world, including aquatic habitats. The following groups are good sources of information. Contact them and ask for material on how you can become involved in their efforts.

NOAA Marine Debris Information Office

The Center for Marine Conservation
1725 De Sales Street NW
Washington, DC 20036
Provides a variety of brochures, posters, and slides about the dangers, and necessary clean-up, of marine pollution. Produces several classroom games, lesson plans, and other free materials.

Throughout the pages of this book you have met some spectacular animals. You've been introduced to an animal that plays with its food while floating on its back, one that drifts across the ocean on a "home-made" raft, another that is jet-propelled, and even one that can swim upside down and backward. The ways in which these creatures swim are part of how they have learned to survive in their special habitat—the water.

An animal's **habitat** is the place where it lives. That place may be a small pond in the mountains, a large expanse of open ocean in the South Pacific, or a rocky shoreline off the California coast. An animal's habitat supplies everything that animal needs for its survival. Those needs may include food, water, light, proper temperature, and some form of protection or shelter from the elements. Oceans, lakes, rivers, and streams are just a few of the special habitats in which animals live.

If an animal's habitat is harmed, destroyed, or polluted, it may mean danger for that animal. It may not be able to locate the food it needs to survive. It may not be able to protect itself from its enemies. It may not be able to mate and reproduce another generation of its kind. The destruction of some habitats is a natural occurrence in nature. In too many cases, however, habitats are threatened or eliminated because of human activity. When oil tankers run aground, the seeping oil threatens hundreds of marine organisms. When ponds and marshes are drained for housing projects, wetland creatures are threatened. When garbage and waste products are dumped into the ocean, fish life may be eliminated.

When an animal's habitat is destroyed, an animal species may be lost forever, never to return. Protecting the habitats of all animals—including surprising swimmers—not only makes sense, but also helps ensure their survival for generations. What we do today has an impact on how well many animals will survive in the future.

Marine Iguanas

International Wildlife Coalition

Whale Adoption Project
634 North Falmouth Highway
Box 388
North Falmouth, MA 02566
Works to preserve the dwindling populations of various whale species. Provides information on how you and your classmates can "adopt" a whale.

National Wildlife Federation

1400 16th Street NW
Washington, DC 20036
Works to preserve and properly manage wildlife resources around the world. A strong advocate of numerous conservation issues.

Preserving animal habitats is a challenge for all humans, but it's a challenge we can meet by working together. I invite you to work with your parents, your teacher, your classmates, and other people in your community. Wherever you live, you can make a difference. Here are some things you may want to consider:

First, look for and learn about the habitats of various aquatic animals in your part of the country. You may wish to read other books like this one or talk with your teacher or parents about the fish, insects, or amphibians that live near you. If possible, you may want to visit one or more of these habitats. Observe, but do not disturb, these animals.

People working together do make a difference! Your interest and enthusiasm can help alert others to important conservation issues. The "surprising swimmers" of the world are counting on you.

My Amazing Animal Adventures

The date of my adventure: _____

The people who came with me: _____

_____

Where I went: _____

What amazing animals I saw:

_____   _____

_____   _____

_____   _____

_____   _____

The date of my adventure: _____

The people who came with me: _____

_____

Where I went: _____

What amazing animals I saw:

_____   _____

_____   _____

_____   _____

_____   _____

TOUGH TERMINATORS

NATURE'S **MOST AMAZING** ANIMALS

Sneed B. Collard III

About Predators

In some science fiction movies, a "terminator" is an awful, computer-controlled robot whose only purpose is to hunt and kill people. Fortunately, there's no such thing as a robot terminator in real life. However, there is a group of living things that survives by hunting and eating animals. They're called **predators**, and they are some of the most amazing creatures on Earth.

At first, it might seem disgusting to think that some animals catch and eat other animals, but there are good reasons why predators live this way. If all life forms ate only plants, there wouldn't be nearly enough food to go around. Meat also provides important nutrients and protein that can be difficult to get from plants. Predation is such a successful way to live that it has evolved in almost every group of animals. As you'll see later in the book, even some *plants* are predators.

DAVID M. DENNIS/TOM STACK AND ASSOCIATES

Predators are essential to life on Earth. They help control the numbers of wild animals, so populations don't overrun their environments. Predators keep wildlife populations healthy by hunting animals that are sick or weak. By eating pests, predators prevent the spread of diseases and reduce damage to crops. All in all, predators help our environment stay balanced and healthy.

People don't always appreciate predators as much as they should. In fact, humans have done their best to hunt and exterminate most of Earth's big predators. Why? For many reasons. One reason is that people are afraid of some predators. A second reason is that predators often compete with people for food by hunting the same animals. But mostly, people have killed predators because they haven't understood the animals very well. Most of the killing isn't necessary. People and predators can almost always live together peacefully.

The following pages contain some of the world's most exciting predators. Prepare to meet 12 "tough terminators" face to face—and to find out how they make our world a better place.

Tiger

Tigers are the world's largest cats. Their sharp teeth are built for stabbing and cutting, while their claws whip in and out like flashing razors. Tigers and other cats belong to the group of mammals called **carnivores**. Carnivores are animals that eat meat.

FAST FACTS

▶ **Scientific Name . . .**
Neofelis tigris
(NEE-OH-FEE-LIS TIE-GRIS)
▶ **Kind of Animal . . .**
Mammal
▶ **Order of Mammals . . .**
Carnivores
▶ **Family of Carnivores . . .**
Felids or "Cats"
▶ **Greatest Weight . . .**
662 pounds
▶ **Greatest Length . . .**
11 feet (from head to tail)
▶ **Lifespan . . .**
12 to 20 years

A tiger usually hunts alone. It can't run very far, so it has to surprise other animals in order to catch them. The tiger sneaks up silently on its prey, then pounces.

Tigers often hunt at night. In the back of their eyes is a mirror-like layer called the **tapetum** (TUH-PEET-UM) that helps tigers—and other nocturnal animals—see in the dark.

LYNN STONE

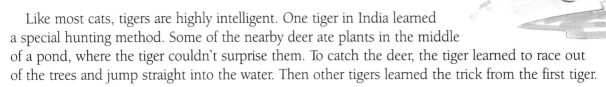

Like most cats, tigers are highly intelligent. One tiger in India learned a special hunting method. Some of the nearby deer ate plants in the middle of a pond, where the tiger couldn't surprise them. To catch the deer, the tiger learned to race out of the trees and jump straight into the water. Then other tigers learned the trick from the first tiger.

To survive, wild tigers need to eat an animal the size of a full-grown deer every two weeks or so. Tigers have been known to attack young elephants and rhinoceroses, but mostly they feed on deer, wild pigs, and smaller animals. To make sure they get enough food, they stake out hunting grounds, or territories. One territory can cover hundreds of square miles.

A hundred years ago, tigers lived from Iran to China and from Siberia to Indonesia. Today, most tigers live in India and southeast Asia.

Tigers are among the few predators that are dangerous to people. During the 1920s, tigers killed about 1,000 people per year in India. Today, tigers kill dozens of people each year in Bangladesh and southeast India. But most tigers avoid humans. Tiger attacks usually happen in places where people have invaded the tiger's territory.

Like most wild cats, the tiger has been relentlessly hunted by people. Expanding human populations have also left few wild places where the tiger can live. To help save the tiger in India, conservation groups and the Indian government started Project Tiger. The project created 19 parks where tigers can live safely and taught the Indian people how to get along with their predator neighbors. Project Tiger has helped India's tiger population double—from 2,000 to about 4,000 animals.

Ladybird Beetle

Predators don't have to be big like the tiger. They don't have to live in wild jungles or forests, either. One of the world's hungriest predators is a small animal you can find in your back yard—the ladybird beetle, or ladybug.

▶ **Kind of Animal . . .**
Insect
▶ **Order of Insects . . .**
Beetles
▶ **Family of Beetles . . .**
Coccinellids or "Ladybird" beetles
▶ **Weight . . .**
Less than 1/100th of an ounce
▶ **Length . . .**
Between .03 and .71 inches
▶ **Lifespan . . .**
One to three years

MARY CLAY/TOM STACK AND ASSOCIATES

The habitats where ladybird beetles live all have one thing in common: food. A few kinds of ladybugs eat leaves and fungus, but most are predators. They catch aphids, mites, and tiny insects called scales.

Like other insects, ladybird beetles live their lives in two major stages. After they hatch from eggs, they are called **larvae** (LAR-VEE). Ladybird beetle larvae look a little like caterpillars. They can't fly like adult beetles can, but they have healthy appetites. A hungry larva can devour 300 aphids in a single day.

As it grows, a larva moults or "sheds its skin" four or five times. After several weeks, it forms a cocoon. Inside this safe refuge, the larva grows into an adult. Like larvae, adult ladybird beetles eat hundreds of aphids and other insects every day.

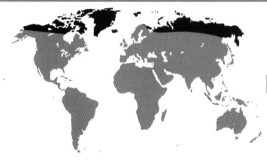

There are over 4,500 species of ladybird beetles. They live all over the world and in many different kinds of places, or habitats.

Where ladybird beetles live

Many predators have powerful eyes and ears to help them find their prey, but not ladybird beetles. Both larvae and adult beetles find other animals by "bumping into" them. Larvae can starve to death if they don't bump into something within a day or two after they hatch. If adults don't find food, they fly to a new plant or a new place and search for food there.

Farmers love ladybird beetles. In the 1890s, Australian ladybird beetles were imported to California so they could eat a kind of scale that was destroying orange trees. The ladybird beetles ate so many that they saved California's citrus industry. Using ladybird beetles and other predators to eat pests helps farmers avoid using dangerous pesticides to protect their crops.

North Pacific Giant Octopus

Like ladybird beetles, octopuses are **invertebrates**—animals without backbones. There are about 200 species of octopuses, but the North Pacific giant octopus is one of the largest.

▶ **Scientific Name . . .**
Enteroctopus dofleini
ENTER-OK-TOH-PUSS DO-FLEEN-EYE

▶ **Kind of Animal . . .**
Cephalopod, or "Head-footed mollusk"

▶ **Order and Family of Cephalopods . . .**
Octopods or "eight-footeds"

▶ **Greatest Weight . . .**
600 pounds

▶ **Greatest Armspan . . .**
31 feet

▶ **Lifespan . . .**
Three to five years

Octopuses are shy, but they're smart. They have the largest brains and are the most intelligent of all invertebrates. In experiments, octopuses have learned how to unscrew the lids of jars so they can reach the food inside.

DAVE B. FLEETHAM/TOM STACK AND ASSOCIATES

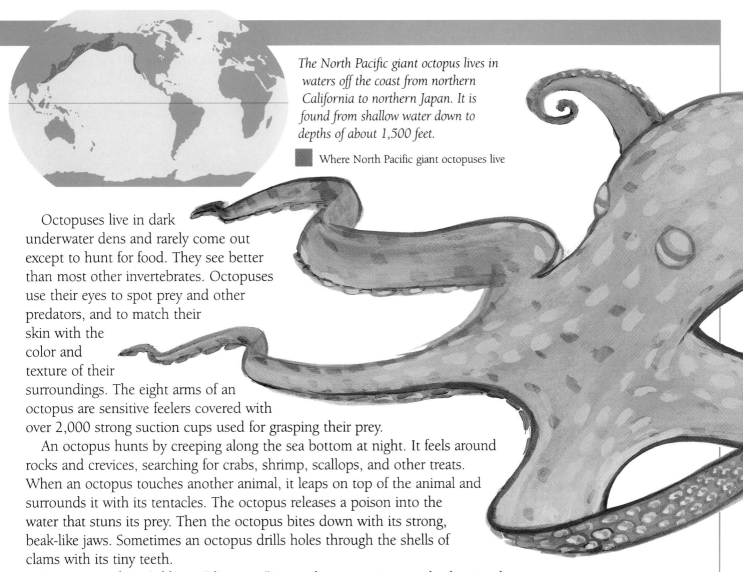

The North Pacific giant octopus lives in waters off the coast from northern California to northern Japan. It is found from shallow water down to depths of about 1,500 feet.

Where North Pacific giant octopuses live

Octopuses live in dark underwater dens and rarely come out except to hunt for food. They see better than most other invertebrates. Octopuses use their eyes to spot prey and other predators, and to match their skin with the color and texture of their surroundings. The eight arms of an octopus are sensitive feelers covered with over 2,000 strong suction cups used for grasping their prey.

An octopus hunts by creeping along the sea bottom at night. It feels around rocks and crevices, searching for crabs, shrimp, scallops, and other treats. When an octopus touches another animal, it leaps on top of the animal and surrounds it with its tentacles. The octopus releases a poison into the water that stuns its prey. Then the octopus bites down with its strong, beak-like jaws. Sometimes an octopus drills holes through the shells of clams with its tiny teeth.

An octopus doesn't like to "dine out." Instead, it carries its prey back to its den. By using its suction cups and the baggy folds of skin between its arms, an octopus can carry up to a dozen crabs at a time.

Many stories have been told about giant octopuses attacking people, but most of these stories are not true. Once in a while a giant octopus will leap onto a scuba diver, but the octopus rarely bites. The animal is usually just curious, and it soon lets go. Most scuba divers feel lucky to be "attacked" by one of the ocean's most intelligent and beautiful predators.

FAST FACTS

Aplomado Falcon

A falcon kills its prey with a flash of silver feathers and a *whack*. Peregrine falcons are famous for their speed—up to 217 miles per hour in a full dive. But another "top gun" that often gets overlooked is the aplomado (AH-PLO-MAH-DOE) falcon.

▶ **Scientific Name . . .**
Falco femoralis
(FAL-KOH FEEM-OR-AL-ISS)
▶ **Kind of Animal . . .**
Bird
▶ **Order of Birds . . .**
Falconiformes or
"Birds of Prey"
▶ **Greatest Weight . . .**
One pound
▶ **Greatest Wingspan . . .**
35 inches
▶ **Lifespan . . .**
12 to 20 years

KENNETH W. FINK/PHOTO RESEARCHERS

The aplomado falcon is a **raptor**, or bird of prey. Raptors include eagles, hawks, ospreys, kites, and falcons. Raptors are the premier hunters of the bird world.

Aplomado is a Spanish word that means "steel gray"— the color of the aplomado's back. Aplomados are not big as raptors go, but their hunting skills are breathtaking.

Like other falcons, aplomados usually hunt birds. An aplomado sits on a tree or a yucca plant, waiting patiently for another bird to come along. When a bird flies nearby, the falcon streaks after it—through trees and brush and across open plains. When it catches up, the falcon slams into the other bird with so much force that the bird's neck may be broken.

Aplomados once lived from the American Southwest all the way to Central America. Now they mostly live in the Mexican states of Veracruz, Tabasco, and Chiapas. A small population exists in Chihuahua and Coahuila.

■ Where aplomado falcons live

Male and female aplomados sometimes hunt together. If they find a bird sitting in a bush or a tree, the male tries to flush out the bird so the female can zoom in for the kill. When aplomados can't find birds to eat, they snatch rodents, lizards, and insects.

Aplomados once lived in Texas, Arizona, and New Mexico. But by 1942, they no longer nested in the U.S. Why? Because most of the open grasslands where falcons like to live had been converted to farms or were overgrown with brush. Pesticides such as DDT weakened the shells of the aplomado's eggs, so they broke before the baby birds could hatch and grow.

Since 1985, a group called The Peregrine Fund has been trying to bring the aplomado back to the Southwest by releasing young falcons. Progress has been slow, but a few aplomados now live in Texas. One day, we may all have the chance to see the brilliant silver flash of one of the Earth's most spectacular raptors.

TERRENCE MOORE

Saltwater Crocodile

- **Species Name . . .**
  Crocodylus porosus
  (KROK-OH-DILL-US POR-OH-SIS)
- **Kind of Animal . . .**
  Reptile
- **Order and Family of Reptiles . . .**
  Crocodiles
- **Greatest Weight . . .**
  Over 6,000 pounds
- **Greatest Length . . .**
  30 feet
- **Lifespan . . .**
  About 65 years

Crocodiles are the closest living relatives to dinosaurs. There are over 20 species of crocodiles, and they are skilled hunters. Most do not bother people. One species that people *should* be careful of is the saltwater crocodile, or "saltie."

JOE McDONALD/TOM STACK AND ASSOCIATES

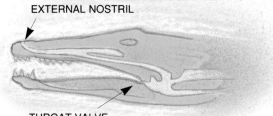

EXTERNAL NOSTRIL

THROAT VALVE

Crocodiles are especially suited to a watery lifestyle. Special valves in their throats keep water from pouring into their lungs when they swallow food or float on the water's surface. They are also excellent swimmers, pushing themselves along with their powerful tails.

Crocodile eyes—like cat eyes—capture extra light for nighttime hunting. Their sensitive ears tell them when even a tiny animal jumps into the water.

Salties eat almost everything. Underwater, they use their spike teeth to catch fish, sharks, turtles, and crabs. Near the shore, they catch monkeys, deer, boars, kangaroos, and even water buffaloes.

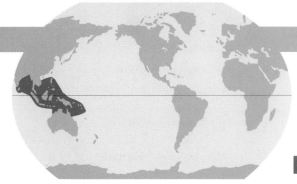

Salties live from southern India to Far East Asia and all the way to Australia. They hang out in swamps, along coasts, or in rivers. However, they sometimes travel hundreds of miles across the open ocean.

■ Where saltwater crocodiles live

Like tigers, salties surprise their prey. Crocodiles drift along, hiding in tall grass or reeds. Sometimes they dive underwater to sneak up on other animals. When they're near the prey animal, they burst out of the water with their teeth flashing. On land, crocodiles can sprint up to 30 miles per hour. They seize their victims in their jaws and swallow small animals in one gulp. Salties drag larger prey animals into deep water to drown them. Then they tear the animals into bite-sized pieces.

The saltwater crocodile is one of the largest and most dangerous of all reptiles. Salties kill several people each year in India, Australia, and New Guinea. In 1975 in Indonesia, crocodiles ate more than 40 people who spilled out of one overturned boat.

DAVE B. FLEETHAM/TOM STACK AND ASSOCIATES

Crocodiles have more to fear from people than we do from them. Salties—and most other crocodiles—have been hunted for their skins. People have made suitcases, handbags, shoes, belts, and even watch straps from the skins. In India and Asia, wild saltwater crocodiles are almost extinct. Salties have a brighter future in New Guinea and Australia, where they are protected by laws and live farther away from people.

Community Spider

- ▶ **Species Name . . .**
  Stegodyphus mimosarum
  (STAY-GO-DIE-FUS MIM-OH-SAIR-UM)
- ▶ **Kind of Animal . . .**
  Arachnid (Spiders, Mites and Scorpions)
- ▶ **Order of Arachnids . . .**
  Spiders
- ▶ **Family of Spiders . . .**
  Eresids
- ▶ **Greatest Weight . . .**
  1/20 of an ounce
- ▶ **Greatest Length . . .**
  4/10 of an inch
- ▶ **Lifespan . . .**
  One year

Without spiders, our planet would soon be overrun by insects and other pests. There may be as many as 180,000 kinds of spiders, and all spiders are carnivorous. A spider usually hunts alone, but about half a dozen species live and hunt together. These are called **social spiders**. One social spider that scientists have studied is the community spider, or *Stegodyphus* (STAY-GO-DIE-FUS).

EDWARD S. ROSS

In Africa, the pea-sized *Stegodyphus* live in shrubs and trees on the open plains. Up to 1,000 *Stegodyphus* spiders may live together. They build huge nests that are made up of **retreats** and webs. Retreats are masses of silk where spiders find shelter. The webs are built to catch the spiders' insect prey. Webs are tough, and they can cover up to four square yards—about the area of a badminton net. By working together to build big webs, the community spiders trap more—and bigger—insects than they could if each one lived alone.

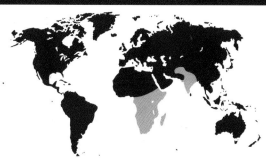

Social spiders are found in South America, Asia, and Australia. Stegodyphus *lives in southern and eastern Africa, Madagascar, and Asia.*

Where community spiders live

Stegodyphus webs trap everything from gnats and ants to wasps and praying mantises. When an insect is caught, it struggles, sending vibrations through the web. If the vibrations are small, only one or two spiders come to investigate. But if the prey is large and thrashing around, dozens of spiders rush out of the retreats.

The spiders kill a trapped insect by biting it and injecting poison into it. Then they begin to feed. Each night the community spiders repair their web in spots where it has been damaged by insects, wind, or rain.

Each *Stegodyphus* spider lives for only about a year, but *Stegodyphus* colonies can last for many years. The colonies benefit over 25 animals besides the community spiders. Several different spider species live with the *Stegodyphus* and steal their food. Wasps and moths lay their eggs on the *Stegodyphus* or in its nests. By working together, community spiders help each other survive, but they also give life to many other animals.

EDWARD S. ROSS

Great Barracuda

The sea—like the land—is a good place to live if you're a predator. You've already seen that octopuses find plenty of slow-moving prey in the ocean. But what about all those speedy ocean fish? Most predators are too slow to catch them, but not the great barracuda.

FAST FACTS

▶ **Species Name . . .**
Sphyraena barracuda
(SFY-REE-NA BEAR-A-COO-DA)

▶ **Kind of Animal . . .**
Fish

▶ **Order of Fishes . . .**
Perciformes or
"Perch-shaped fish"

▶ **Family of Perciformes . . .**
Sphyraenids or "Barracudas"

▶ **Greatest Weight . . .**
106 pounds

▶ **Greatest Length . . .**
6 feet

▶ **Lifespan . . .**
15 years

Barracudas hunt during the day. Like some sharks, they make their living by catching other fish. Young barracudas live in grassbeds and eat small fish like gobies and sardines.

By the time they are one or two feet long, barracudas stake out territories in shallow water. During most of the day, each barracuda hunts alone within its territory, which might cover several hundred square feet. When the tide comes in, though, medium-sized barracudas band together. Working as a team, they attack incoming schools of fish. When they grow larger, barracudas stop working together. Large barracudas are loners, patrolling deeper waters for puffers, needlefish, and other "fish dinners."

MIKE BACON/TOM STACK AND ASSOCIATES

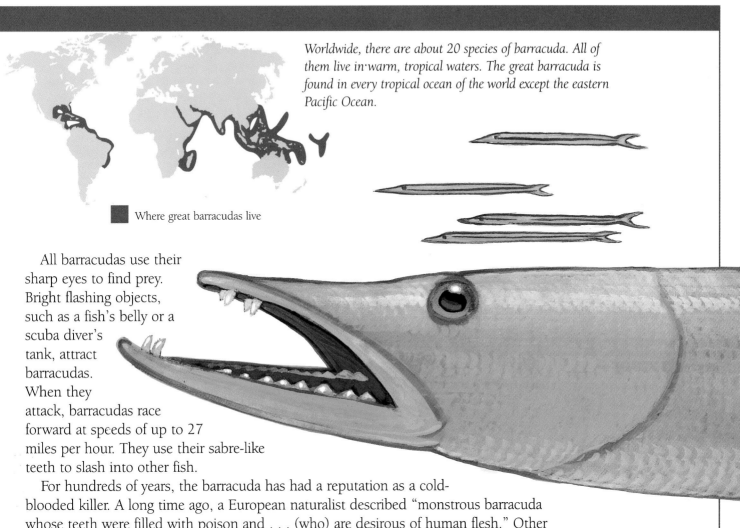

Worldwide, there are about 20 species of barracuda. All of them live in warm, tropical waters. The great barracuda is found in every tropical ocean of the world except the eastern Pacific Ocean.

Where great barracudas live

All barracudas use their sharp eyes to find prey. Bright flashing objects, such as a fish's belly or a scuba diver's tank, attract barracudas. When they attack, barracudas race forward at speeds of up to 27 miles per hour. They use their sabre-like teeth to slash into other fish.

For hundreds of years, the barracuda has had a reputation as a cold-blooded killer. A long time ago, a European naturalist described "monstrous barracuda whose teeth were filled with poison and . . . (who) are desirous of human flesh." Other people told stories of 20-foot-long barracudas that attacked men, dogs, and horses. Today we know that these reports were exaggerated. In the past 100 years, only about 35 barracuda attacks have been confirmed, and just one victim died from the attack.

By the way, eating barracudas can be dangerous. The meat from barracudas and many other tropical fish can contain a poison called **ciguatera** (SIG-WA-TAIR-UH) toxin. There is no way to know which fish are poisonous and which are not. This is too bad for seafood lovers who would like to eat a barracuda steak, but it's extra protection for the barracuda.

Pitcher Plant

FAST FACTS

▶ **Kind of Plant . . .**
Flowering plant
▶ **Order and Family of Flowering Plants . . .**
New World Pitcher Plants
▶ **Greatest Height . . .**
Four feet
▶ **Lifespan . . .**
10 to 30 years

By now you're probably getting the idea that being a predator is a successful way to live. If they could talk, some plants would agree. These plants are called **insectivorous** plants, because they trap and eat insects and other small animals. One especially clever insectivore is the pitcher plant.

KERRY T. GIVENS/TOM STACK AND ASSOCIATES

Pitcher plants live in bogs, swamps, and other wet places where the soil is too poor for other plants. But pitcher plants *thrive* here. Why? Because other plants need to obtain nutrients from the soil, but the pitcher plant "steals" nitrogen and other nutrients from the insects it catches. And there are plenty of insects in wet places.

Pitcher plants catch insects in wonderful ways. Their leaves are shaped into modified traps called pitchers. Sweet-smelling nectar glands serve as bait for the unsuspecting prey.

Where New World pitcher plants live

New World pitcher plants live in North and South America. We are lucky to have about ten species of pitcher plants in the United States and Canada. Most live in the southeastern U.S.

JOHN GERLACH/TOM STACK AND ASSOCIATES

The nectar glands are concentrated near the mouth of the pitcher. Flies, moths, mosquitoes, and ants can't resist this sweet meal. When the insects get to the top of the plant, watch out! The rim and the inside surface are coated with a slippery, waxy substance. If the insect makes one false move, it's plunged into the pitcher, where it's digested in a pool of juices.

Pitcher plants are harmless to people, but they help control pests by catching hundreds of kinds of insects. Each fall, the pitchers and the flowers of the plant wither away. But the roots may live for decades, sending up fresh pitchers and flowers every spring.

Several varieties of pitcher plants are common, but others are rare and endangered. Many wet places where pitcher plants grow have been drained for building and farming. Plant collectors also dig up pitcher plants. The U.S. Fish and Wildlife Service and conservation groups are working hard to make sure that these precious plant predators survive.

117

Siphonophore

Sharks and barracudas get more attention, but siphonophores (SY-FAHN-O-FORZ) may be the most important predators in the sea. Siphonophores belong to a group of animals known as **gelatinous zooplankton**, or "jelly animals." These are soft-bodied, jellyfish-like creatures that are carried around by ocean currents.

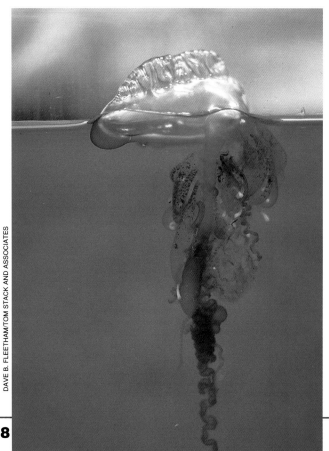

DAVE B. FLEETHAM/TOM STACK AND ASSOCIATES

People often call a siphonophore an animal, but it's really a collection or colony of little animals that work together. Some parts of the colony are good at swimming. Other parts are good at catching or digesting food. Still others specialize in reproduction.

Siphonophores hunt by using a "sit-in-waiting" strategy. A typical siphonophore stretches its body and extends dozens or even thousands of tentacles. These tentacles are often loaded with stinging cells called **nematocysts** (NEE-MAT-O-SISTS), which can stun or kill the siphonophore's prey.

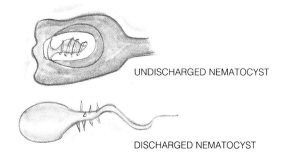

UNDISCHARGED NEMATOCYST

DISCHARGED NEMATOCYST

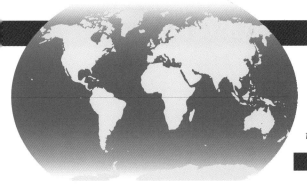

Siphonophores live in all the world's oceans. There are over 160 species, and they live from the ocean surface to depths of more than 12,000 feet.

■ Where siphonophores live

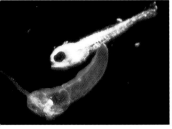

To help attract prey, some of the siphonophore's tentacles contain tiny parts that look like fish, shrimp, or jellyfish. By dangling and jiggling these "decoys," the siphonophore lures fish and other animals to their death.

Most siphonophores are small, but some reach enormous sizes. One called *Apolemia* is hundreds of feet long. It may even be the longest "animal" (or colony) in the world. When *Apolemia* hangs out its tentacles, it becomes a "wall of death" that traps thousands of animals.

Top: "Decoy" and fish larva.
Bottom: Apolemia.

The most famous kind of siphonophore is the Portugese Man-of-War, which lives in all of the world's tropical seas. The Portugese Man-of-War and several other siphonophores can deliver a powerful sting, but they're not considered deadly to people.

119

Gray Wolf

FAST FACTS

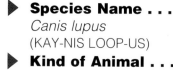

- ▶ **Species Name . . .**
  Canis lupus
  (KAY-NIS LOOP-US)
- ▶ **Kind of Animal . . .**
  Mammal
- ▶ **Order of Mammals . . .**
  Carnivores
- ▶ **Family of Carnivores . . .**
  Canids or "Dogs"
- ▶ **Weight . . .**
  33 to 176 pounds
- ▶ **Length . . .**
  4 to 6 feet
- ▶ **Lifespan . . .**
  8 to 20 years

No other "terminator" has inspired more fear than the wolf. In stories like "Little Red Riding Hood," wolves are villains that attack grandmothers and devour small children. But in recent times, people have discovered that wolves are not such bad guys after all.

TOM AND PAT LEESON

Wolves eat different things, depending on where they live. In desert areas, they pounce on rabbits and other small prey. Where larger prey is common, wolves hunt moose, beaver, and caribou. But wolves are fairly small, and they're not fast runners. In order to kill large animals, they often hunt in social groups called **packs**.

Each wolf pack contains between two and 20 wolves. The pack is highly organized, and it's led by two wolves—the **alpha male** and the **alpha female**. The two alpha wolves are usually the only pack members that mate, and they also lead the pack in hunting and feeding. To catch a caribou or a moose, several wolves may rush at the animal and overwhelm it. At other times, one or two wolves may trap an animal by herding it toward other wolves.

Wolves once roamed over most of the northern hemisphere—from the Arctic Circle to Mexico and even the deserts of the Middle East. Today, large wolf populations are found only in parts of Canada, Alaska, Minnesota, Iran, southeastern Europe, and the former Soviet Union.

◼ Former wolf range

◼ Current wolf range

Like many other predators, wolves are highly intelligent. They howl to stay in touch with each other. Younger wolves learn how and where to hunt from older wolves in the pack. As long ago as 10,000 years, people learned that they could tame and breed wolves as workers and companions. All modern dogs—from poodles to German shepherds—are descended from the tamed wolves of long ago.

There are hundreds of stories about wolves attacking and killing people. Almost all of these stories are false. Probably the biggest reason people have feared wolves is because wolves compete with us as predators. Wolves eat deer that hunters would like to shoot for themselves. Sometimes wolves feed on domestic livestock. They don't know that cows belong to a rancher or dairy farmer. To wolves, a cow simply looks like dinner.

But people and wolves can—and do—live together peacefully. Over a thousand wolves live in Minnesota, many of them near farms. In Italy, wolves live within 30 miles of Rome, a city of almost three million people. When people start to understand these predators, they realize that wolves are really shy, intelligent, and amazing animals.

TOM AND PAT LEESON

Dragonfly

- ▶ **Kind of Animal . . .**
  Insect
- ▶ **Order of Insects . . .**
  Odonata or "Dragonfly"
  or "Darner"
- ▶ **Weight . . .**
  Less than an ounce
- ▶ **Wingspan . . .**
  Up to seven inches
- ▶ **Lifespan . . .**
  Up to six years as larva,
  then 40 to 50 days as adult

Dragonflies are one of the oldest groups of insects. Naturalists have found fossils of primitive dragonflies that are over 200 million years old. Some of these dragonflies had wingspans of 28 inches—the same wingspan as a small, modern-day duck or hawk.

JOHN GERLACH/TOM STACK AND ASSOCIATES

Like ladybird beetles, dragonflies are predators in both their larval and adult stages. But unlike the ladybugs, dragonflies are **opportunistic hunters**. They eat almost anything they can catch.

Dragonflies spend most of their lives as aquatic larvae, living in ponds, streams, and lakes. They moult up to 15 times, shedding their skins and growing bigger with each moult. After their final moult, they climb out of the water as adults.

Adult dragonflies may be the most spectacular fliers in the insect world. They have two pairs of wings that beat independently, allowing them to fly forward, sideways, and even backward.

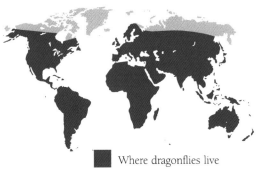

Where dragonflies live

There are over 5,000 species of dragonflies. They're most common in the tropics and near wetlands, but they live in many habitats—from deserts to high mountains to polar regions.

FLY EATING CONTEST

To help them spot their prey, dragonflies have two large eyes called "compound eyes." Each compound eye contains thousands of little eyes that give dragonflies an almost 360-degree view of their environment. Dragonflies also have three small eyes called "ocelli" on the upper parts of their heads. Ocelli do not focus on objects, but they seem to tell dragonflies how much light is around them and which way is up.

Dragonflies hunt by patrolling the air for prey or by "perching and waiting" on grasses or rocks. When a dragonfly sees something it wants to eat, it zooms forward and crashes into its prey at speeds of up to 30 miles per hour. The dragonfly captures the prey animal in a "basket" that it forms with its legs. Then it devours the animal in mid-air.

Dragonflies eat many kinds of animals that are harmful to people, including tsetse flies, horseflies, mosquitoes, aphids, and locusts. One hungry dragonfly can catch about 200 of these animals in one day.

Artists, insect collectors, and scientists have been fascinated by dragonflies for hundreds of years. But water pollution and the draining of marshes and lakes have destroyed many dragonfly homes. If these fabulous fliers are to survive for another 200 million years, we must protect our marshes, lakes, and other wetlands.

Gray Whale

We don't usually think of large whales as predators. That's because big whales like the gray whale have **baleen** in their mouths instead of teeth. A whale's baleen looks like an enormous comb that fills the whale's mouth. It acts like a huge trap, and the large whales use it to catch more animals than any other kind of predator.

FAST FACTS

- **Species Name . . .**
  Eschrichtius robustus
  (ESH-RIK-TEE-US ROW-BUST-US)
- **Kind of Animal . . .**
  Mammal
- **Order of Mammals . . .**
  Cetaceans or "Whales and Porpoises"
- **Greatest Weight . . .**
  75,000 pounds
- **Greatest Length . . .**
  49 feet
- **Greatest Lifespan . . .**
  56 years

JAMES D. WATT/PACIFIC STOCK

Most baleen whales "filter" water through their mouths to find shrimp and other kinds of food. Gray whales feed this way, but they also eat in another way.

Unlike other whales, gray whales "graze" like deep-sea cattle along muddy sea bottoms. They dive as deep as 200 feet, then roll on their sides. When they open their mouths, they turn into the world's biggest vacuum cleaners, sucking up hundreds of pounds of mud in an instant.

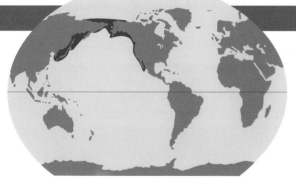

Gray whales used to live in the Atlantic and Pacific Oceans. By about the year 1700, however, Europeans had hunted Atlantic gray whales to extinction. Most gray whales now live along the western (Pacific) coast of North America.

■ Where gray whales live today

Gray whales sift through the mud for worms, crustaceans, and other invertebrates. When they've caught enough invertebrates in their baleen, the whales slurp them down with the help of their six-foot tongues. One scientist estimated that a gray whale can eat over 150,000 pounds of invertebrates in a single summer. Since most of the invertebrates weigh an ounce or less, that's a lot of sifting and grazing.

Gray whales spend their winters in Mexico, where they give birth to baby gray whales. The whales don't eat much during the winter, because food supplies are not as abundant and the whales are busy mating, giving birth, and raising their young. In spring, though, they migrate north like many birds do. In the shallow Arctic seas near Alaska, the feasting really starts. During a single summer, an adult gray whale might gain over 12,000 pounds.

Many people think that gray whales are the smartest whales of all. Whalers called them "devil fish" because their boats were often attacked by gray whales. When they're being chased, gray whales change speed, dive, and use other tricks to escape.

Whalers killed up to three-quarters of all the Pacific gray whales by the late 1800s. Fortunately, gray whales were protected by law in 1946, and today there may be more Pacific gray whales than ever. Over 20,000 grazing gray predators migrate up and down the Pacific coastline each year.

Protecting Tough Terminators

The Nature Conservancy
1815 North Lynne Street
Arlington, VA 22209
(Protects predators, plants, and animals
by safeguarding lands and waters)

Greenpeace Public Information
1436 U Street NW
Washington, D.C. 20009
(Works on many environmental issues,
including protection of whales and oceans)

U.S. Fish and Wildlife Service
Publications Unit
4401 North Fairfax Drive
Mail Stop 130 Webb
Arlington, VA 22203
(Works to protect endangered species,
including gray wolves and falcons)

Sierra Club
Public Affairs Department
730 Polk Street
San Francisco, CA 94109
(Works on many environmental issues,
including protection of predators and
endangered species)

**The Peregrine Fund
Interpretive Center**
5666 West Flying Hawk Lane
Boise, ID 83709
(Works to bring falcons back to their
former homes and protects other birds
of prey)

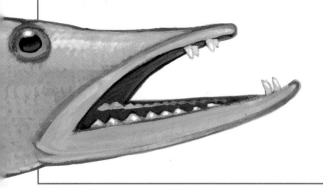

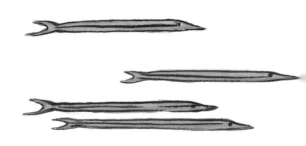

The Top Predator

By now you know a lot about predators. You've seen how predators hunt, what they eat, and where they live. But there's one group of predators we haven't talked about. They are the most important predators of all: people.

People eat many kinds of food, but for thousands of years we have eaten other animals in order to survive. Some "people predators" have hunted in forests and deserts. Other people predators have raised their own prey animals, like goats, cows, and chickens. Still others have fished the oceans and lakes for food.

Being predators has helped us survive, but our activities have also affected the earth and its creatures. Hunting has driven many species—including other predators—to extinction. By grazing on grasses, the sheep, cows, and goats we raise have turned some fertile grasslands into deserts. Overfishing has destroyed food sources in many areas. Even cats and dogs—our "pet predators"—have wiped out wildlife in some areas. On one island in New Zealand, a lighthouse keeper's cat eliminated 13 species of birds from the island.

Because we are the world's "top predators," we are the only ones who can make sure our planet remains a great place to live. We can do many things to keep our environment healthy, and one of the most important is to help other predators survive. To help small predators like ladybird beetles and dragonflies, we can keep a pond in the back yard or avoid spraying pesticides on the lawn.

To help larger predators, you can share what you've learned about them with your family and friends. You can also get more information about helping predators by writing to the groups listed on the next page. Remember that predators— whether they're people, animals, or plants—are more than tough. They're terrific!

LARRY MISHKAR

My Amazing Animal Adventures

The date of my adventure: _____

The people who came with me: _____

_____

Where I went: _____

What amazing animals I saw:

_____   _____

_____   _____

_____   _____

_____   _____

The date of my adventure: _____

The people who came with me: _____

_____

Where I went: _____

What amazing animals I saw:

_____   _____

_____   _____

_____   _____

_____   _____

WEIRD WALKERS

NATURE'S MOST AMAZING ANIMALS
Anthony D. Fredericks

About Walkers

Starfish

How do you walk? Like many people, you put one foot in front of the other, lift the back foot, and move it ahead of the one on the ground. Then you repeat the action. The motion is not complex.

It's something you do every day. It's also an efficient way of getting from one place to another.

Mangrove trees

Walking is a form of **locomotion** (or travel) that allows an organism, such as yourself, to move through its environment. The distance traveled may be a few inches a day or many miles a week. Many species use walking as a way to search for food, to seek shelter, or to locate potential mates for breeding. Some species combine walking with other forms of locomotion such as running, flying, or swimming. How and why an organism walks is related to its lifestyle and its survival needs. Many organisms have specialized forms of walking that make them unique. Some organisms can walk straight up trees. Other organisms can walk backward. A few can walk upside down. There is an incredible number of walking methods, each different from the way *you* typically walk.

In this book you will discover some of the most unusual walkers on our planet. You'll learn about a fish that walks *out* of the water, a lizard that walks *on* the water, and even a tree that "walks" *through* the water. As you read, think about how these forms of locomotion are similar to, or different from, the way you walk, skip, or run. How and where an organism walks is part of how it has been able to adapt to its environment. You will be surprised to discover that the act of walking, for many organisms, may be more complex than you originally thought.

MUDSKIPPERS

Mudskippers are members of the Goby family, a group of fish whose pectoral fins are shaped like suckers—allowing them to cling to rocks and other slippery surfaces. Mudskippers live in mangrove swamps and mudflats from West Africa to Southeast Asia and the Southwest Pacific Ocean. They range from 5 to 12 inches long and look like tadpoles with very large heads. Their "pop-eyes" are their most distinctive physical feature.

Startling Steppers

When we think of fish, we usually think about creatures that glide through the ocean or swim in a lake. But there's one fish that spends most of its time out of water and, oddly enough, most of its time climbing trees—it's the mudskipper.

This unique fish has specially developed fins which allow it to walk across the mudflats of seashores and rivers and climb up the trunks of mangrove trees. The **pectoral fins** are on the front of the mudskipper. They are very large and are similar to the limbs of a land animal. The **pelvic fins** are on the back of this fish. They are joined together to form a modified sucker used for grasping limbs and branches.

Although it's an ocean creature, the mudskipper frequently swims to shore. There, it leaps onto the beach and begins to walk by pulling itself along with its front fins. This walking motion makes it look like a miniature seal. An entire school of mudskippers "walking" along the shoreline is quite an amazing sight!

When it's hungry for insects, its favorite food, a mudskipper approaches a limb or tree trunk.

It pulls itself up the trunk with its front fins and holds on with its back fins. It is able to climb a short distance up the tree. These fish also "skip" along the mudflats as they move from one tree to another. By quickly pushing their tails against the sand or mud, mudskippers can travel quite rapidly across the beach.

Although mudskippers spend a lot of time out of the water, they need to keep their skin moist. Occasionally, they will hop off their branches, walk across the sand, and jump into small tidal pools to wet their skin. Mudskippers need to keep their eyes wet, too. To do that, they often pull their eyes back into their head (they don't have tear ducts like you). Mudskippers' eyes can move in all directions—searching for insects while watching for other fish that might invade their territory.

Mudskippers are also unusual because they are one of the few fish able to breathe on land as well as in the water. In the water, mudskippers use their gills just like other fish. This allows them to take in oxygen from the surrounding water. On land, mudskippers are able to breathe because of a special series of membranes lining the back of their mouths and throats. These membranes are richly supplied with a network of blood vessels, allow-ing mudskippers to absorb oxygen directly from the air. A fish that can breathe oxygen and walk up the trunks of trees is an example of adaptation—a physical feature or behavioral trait that has changed over time to improve an organism's chance for survival. The wide variety of plants and animals with which we live and the uncommon ways they live are exciting areas for exploration.

Fantastic Fact

In one species of mudskipper, the male fish do "push-ups" on the sand with their pectoral fins. This helps them attract females.

MILLIPEDES

Millipedes are some of the most ancient of land animals. Most millipedes are small (about 1 inch or so) and are brown or black. Other varieties are large and come in a rainbow of colors, including red and orange. They can be found inside houses, under rocks, in cracks, and in leaf mold. They don't like light so they prefer to hide in dark places. Millipedes are found throughout the world.

Lots O' Legs

How would you walk if you had eight legs? How about 80 legs? How about 200 legs? How would you coordinate all those legs so that you could be able to move forward and not trip over a dozen or more of your own legs?

The millipede is a remarkable animal simply because of all its legs. The word millipede actually means thousand-footed, but no millipede has 1,000 feet. There are about 7,500 species of millipedes throughout the world. Some have as few as 20 legs, while a few tropical species have as many as 230 legs.

Oddly enough, most millipedes are clumsy and slow. Their legs are designed for moving through loose soil and **humus** (decaying matter on the ground) rather than scurrying out in the open. They are more at home pushing their way through the top layers of dirt and soil. Some millipedes however, are **predators** (animals that hunt and eat other animals). They can move rapidly when attacking their prey.

Because centipedes also have a lot of legs, many people confuse millipedes with centipedes, when in fact, they are not related at all. Centipedes (often referred to as "hundred-leggers") have one pair of legs per body segment and typically move in an S-shaped pattern. Millipedes, with two pairs of legs on each body segment, move in a straight line without wiggling.

Centipedes also have longer legs than millipedes, with the legs in the back longer than those in the front. The legs of millipedes are all the same size. Even though millipedes have many more legs than centipedes, they walk much slower.

Millipedes have round heads with a pair of short antennae. When disturbed, they coil up into a tight protective ball so that their enemies cannot get at them.

Several varieties of tropical millipedes give off a foul odor when they are disturbed. They do this through a series of stink glands located along both sides of their bodies. The fluid produced by these glands can, in some species, be sprayed for a distance of more than 2 feet. The fluid contains cyanide, a poison that temporarily blinds or injures any enemy seeking to make the millipede a meal. The millipede then has time to escape into the soil or surrounding plant life.

Fantastic Fact

One species of tropical millipede grows up to 11 inches long. When it is disturbed it coils up into a ball the size of a golf ball.

Twig Travelers

Walk through any tropical rain forest in Central or South America and look up in the branches of the overhanging trees. If you look carefully you may be able to locate some of the prettiest and most distinctive inhabitants of this ecosystem—tree frogs.

Tree frogs spend their entire lives in trees, seldom coming down to the ground. In fact, they eat, sleep, travel, and even lay their eggs high up in the branches of trees. Generally small with slender legs, they have sticky round toe pads on their feet which allow them to walk over, under, around, and upside down through the branches and leaves of rain forest trees. Their toe pads are so sticky that a tree frog can walk straight up a sheet of glass!

We often think of frogs as good leapers and jumpers; however, tree frogs walk much better than they can jump. The only time they do jump is when an unsuspecting insect or other tasty morsel flies by.

Tree frogs come in all colors of the rainbow. European frogs are green, strawberry-poison-dart frogs are red, banana tree frogs are brown, yellow reed frogs are yellow, and poison-dart frogs are blue. There's even a tree frog that is transparent—the glass frog. You can see right through its skin and watch its heart beat!

One of the best known tree frogs of the rain forest is the red-eyed tree frog. This colorful creature is nocturnal, awake and hunting during the night and sleeping during the day. Its most distinguishing feature is its big red eyes, which it uses to seek out food during its nightly hunts. It's also noted for laying its eggs under leaves that

Frogs do not drink water— they absorb it through their skin.

hang out over small ponds or streams. As the eggs hatch, the tadpoles fall into the water below. There, they develop into frogs. Then, they will walk straight up into the trees where they spend the remainder of their lives.

One of the well-known tree frogs in the United States is the common gray tree frog. This frog has an ability to change color depending on its surroundings. Like a chameleon, the cells of its skin move, making the color change. If it is walking along green plants, its skin will be green. If it is resting or crawling on the bark of a tree, its skin will turn brown. Often called a "tree toad" its small size (1 to 2 inches) and coloring makes it difficult to locate.

OSTRICHES

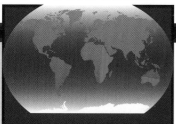

Rapid Runners

Ostriches can be found principally in eastern Africa and a few places in southern Australia. They enjoy living in dry areas and will often move about in large groups. In desert areas, they get their water by eating succulent plants. They also eat large amounts of sand to help them digest their food. Despite what many people think, they do not hide their heads in the sand.

Birds are animals that fly through the air with the greatest of ease. Eagles swoop and dive from great distances, sea gulls soar lazily over ocean waves, and robins dart through the trees around our homes. But have you ever seen a bird that *cannot* fly—a bird that spends its entire life walking or running—never flying?

Fantastic Fact

More than 5,000 humming-bird eggs (the world's smallest eggs) can fit inside *one* ostrich egg—the world's largest egg.

Ostriches are part of a group of birds known as flightless birds. These include Australian emus, New Guinea cassowaries, and New Zealand kiwis. Flightless birds make up less than 1 percent of all the birds in the world, but they also represent one-third of the 75 or more bird species that have become extinct (they no longer exist) over the past 400 years.

Ostriches are the world's tallest birds—males often grow to heights of 9 feet (half of that height is the bird's neck). Ostriches may weigh up to 330 pounds or more. Yet, in spite of their size, these birds are fast runners.

An adult ostrich can run as fast as 45 mph, but will often "cruise" at a steady speed of 31 mph over long stretches of flat land. Newborn ostrich chicks can run soon after they hatch. In a month, they can reach speeds of up to 35 mph.

When ostriches are chased by other animals, they don't run away. For some unknown reason, they just run around in a circle. If caught, ostriches will fight with their feet, both of which have two strong toes. The longest toe on each foot is armed with a sharp claw that can quickly injure any attacking enemy.

Ostriches like to mingle with other animals such as zebras and antelopes.

These animals kick up insects and other small animals that the ostriches like to eat. Because the ostriches are so tall, they can see approaching enemies and sound an "alarm" for their companions. By living together, several different animals can benefit one another.

Female ostriches lay 6 to 8 eggs at one time. Each of these eggs is 6 inches long and may weigh up to 2 pounds.

During the day, the female ostriches sit on the eggs. At night, the males incubate the eggs (keep them warm). After hatching, baby ostriches grow rapidly, reaching a height of 6 feet in six months.

Although ostriches cannot fly, they can travel faster than many other types of birds. This ability helps the ostrich live in its environment and escape from its enemies. It's one way the ostrich has been able to adapt to its surroundings.

Tumbling Tentacles

Hydras can be found throughout the world, with about ten species living in the United States. Tan, gray, or brown in color, they are related to jellyfish, sea anemones, and corals. One species of hydra—*Chlorohydra viridissima*—has single-celled algae living in its cells, giving the hydra its greenish color.

It's a flower that stings! It's a creature that eats its victims whole! And it's an organism that somersaults across the floor of a pond! What is it? A hydra.

Hydras can be found growing on sticks, stones, or water plants in all types of freshwater. Shaped like thin cylinders, they are approximately 1/4 to 1/2 inch long. At first glance, they look more like flowers than animals. One end of a hydra is surrounded by five to seven tentacles (long, thin arms), which can stretch out to make the hydra look like a long thread or pull back so that the hydra looks like a small egg.

Primarily, hydras use their tentacles to capture and eat small water creatures. Each tentacle has tiny cells that contain stinging threads. The threads are driven into an unsuspecting animal and a poison is released that paralyzes the victim. The entire meal is slowly pulled into the hydra's mouth to be digested whole.

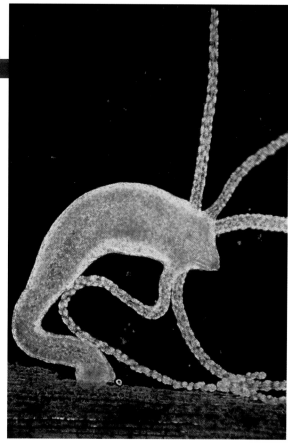

Although hydras usually stay attached in one place for long periods of time, they also "walk" across the floor of a lake. To do this the hydra leans over and grips the surface with its tentacles. Then it somersaults into a new position. Can you imagine walking to school by somersaulting all the way there?

Hydras can reproduce through a process known as **budding**. From time to time small knobs appear on the surface of a hydra. As the buds grow, they begin to develop tentacles. When completely developed, the new organism breaks off and begins its life as an independent creature.

Although hydras have an unusual way of "walking," this method of locomotion helps them survive in their environment. In moving about, hydras can locate new sources of food as well as new areas in which to live.

Fantastic Fact

Hydras can regenerate (re-grow) and replace all their body cells in a period of several weeks.

MEASURING WORMS

There are thousands of species of measuring worms found throughout the United States and Canada, and Europe and Asia. There are about 1,200 species just in the United States. While many species, such as cankerworms, damage fruit and shade trees, others, such as cabbage loopers, are responsible for serious damage to vegetables and other crops.

Inching Insects

Here's an animal that not only walks strangely, it stands still in an unusual way, too. Some people call it a measuring worm, others refer to it as an inchworm, looper, or spanworm. But whatever name it goes by, it certainly travels in a distinctive manner.

If you look closely at a measuring worm, the first thing you notice is that it doesn't have any legs in the middle of its body. It has three pairs of tiny legs called **prolegs** on the front of its body and two or three sets of prolegs on the rear of its body. When it walks along a branch, it pulls the back part of its body up toward the front part, creating a hump in the middle. Then it grasps the surface of the branch tightly with its rear legs and extends the front part forward. It holds onto the surface with its front legs, releases its back legs, and humps up its middle—beginning the process all over again. When a measuring worm goes out for a walk, it looks like it is "inching" along, or carefully measuring the surface on which it walks. This is how it got its name.

a measuring worm and never notice it was a live animal. Measuring worms eat lots of vegetation—especially the leaves of trees. Thus, they are a serious pest of fruit farmers. After a measuring worm has finished its meal in one tree, it will quickly drop down from the branches of that tree on a long silken thread. The thread is spun in a manner similar to that of silkworms. Special glands near the worm's lower jaw give off a fluid that hardens into a fine thread as soon as it hits the air. One end of the thread is fastened to a branch or twig and the worm slides down this "ladder" to the ground.

When it reaches the ground it will "inch" along to other vegetation or another tree to begin eating again.

A measuring worm spends much of its life eating and will consume its own weight in leaves in a single day.

Not only is the measuring worm a weird walker, it is also a "weird stander." Whenever a measuring worm feels threatened by an enemy, it "locks" itself into an upright position and remains motionless on a twig. It looks exactly like part of a twig or branch, standing still for hours until the danger passes. In fact, you could look right at

MANGROVE TREES

Creeping Crawlers

Plants can't walk, right? Well, technically, plants can't really walk, because walking means the ability to propel oneself by physically moving one or more body parts, usually the feet. And since most plants are firmly anchored into the ground by roots, they can't really walk like an insect or a frog or you. But let's meet a plant many people refer to as the "walking tree"—the mangrove tree.

A mangrove tree doesn't grow on land, but in shallow water along the shoreline. It does, however, help create land in several unusual ways. First, the mangrove tree is able to bloom throughout the year—its seeds appearing up and down its branches. Second, a root begins to grow from each seed while it's still on the tree. These roots may often grow to 1 foot in length. Eventually the seeds drop off the tree and into the surrounding water. The seeds may float away during high tide or stick into the mud during periods of low tide. Soon a new tree begins to grow, sending out spidery prop roots from its stem. In fact, a mangrove tree looks like a tall bush

Under the proper conditions, the "legs" of a mangrove tree can grow as fast as 1 inch every hour— that's two feet a day!

with many spidery legs sticking out in all directions.

As the roots of several mangrove trees grow, they become entangled with one another. Sand and dirt become trapped in the roots and soil begins to build up around them. Eventually, so much sand and mud form around the many roots that the tree is no longer in the water—it's on land!

Areas of mangrove trees are an important habitat for a wide variety of wildlife. Small fish, crabs, and other marine organisms use the roots as their home and as a place to obtain the food they need to survive. Birds use mangrove trees to build their nests and raise their young. Mangrove trees also prevent excessive loss of shorelines and beaches. By holding in the sand and

mud, they help reduce the amount of shoreline erosion (land that is worn and washed away) caused by waves, tides, and storms.

Mangrove trees never stop growing and they are continually spreading. Many mangrove seeds float to new areas, take root, and start new "islands." They continue to send out their spidery roots, making it seem as though whole groves of trees are "walking" out to sea. If you could take a series of photographs over a period of several months, you would be able to see how mangrove trees "walk" across large stretches of shallow water.

STARFISH

In some parts of the world, starfish are a major ecological problem. Since they enjoy eating mollusks, such as coral, they can be found in great numbers throughout the world and along many of the world's most beautiful coral reefs, such as the Great Barrier Reef of Australia. There, they are destroying large sections of the reef. Portions of this reef, which have been built up over hundreds of years, are being forever lost to starfish.

Sea Strollers

Found in all the oceans of the world, starfish are some of nature's most incredible creatures. There are more than 5,000 species of starfish—with some of the most unusual found in tropical waters. Starfish can have as few as four arms or as many as 50. At the end of each arm is a small red "eye" that is only able to sense light and dark. Starfish will range in size from as small as 1/2 inch across to others 3 feet in diameter.

Starfish move by means of numerous **tube feet** located on the underside of each arm. The tube feet are hollow muscular cylinders filled with water. When starfish walk, the "feet" are pushed out hydraulically by the contraction of muscular sacs. At the tips of the feet are suction discs which help starfish stick to rocks or prey. Starfish walk by fixing their suckers to the rocks and then pulling themselves forward.

In several species, one of the starfish's arms nearly always takes the lead when the starfish is walking. In other species, it is more usual for the arms to "take turns" in leading the way. The typical speed for a starfish is about 2 to 3 inches a minute.

One amazing feature of the starfish is its ability to regenerate lost arms. If an arm is pulled off or is damaged in some way, the starfish can grow a new arm over a period of several weeks. Some starfish can lose all their arms but one and not only survive, but regenerate all the missing arms.

Even though starfish do not have any teeth, they are **carnivorous** animals

Fantastic Fact

The Linckia starfish is able to pull itself in separate directions until it breaks into two parts. Each of the two parts can grow into a new animal.

(meat-eaters). Typically, they feed on clams, mollusks, worms, crustaceans, oysters, and fish. Shellfish are their favorite food, however. They eat clams and oysters by positioning themselves over the shell of their meal. Gripping a nearby rock with some of their suckers, they hold on to both halves of the oyster's or clam's shell with other suckers. Then they begin to pull the

two shell halves apart. Because of the clam's strong muscles, a starfish may need to pull for several hours or even several days before it can separate the shell halves. The starfish then pushes its stomach into the shellfish, inserting it inside out. The starfish secretes digestive juices into the unlucky mollusk and digests it right inside its own shell. Starfish are one of the few animals that can push their stomachs out of their bodies and turn them inside out to eat a meal. How do you think you would look with your stomach outside your body?

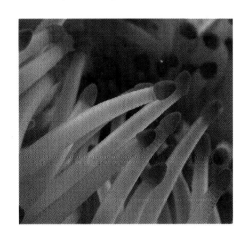

BASILISK LIZARDS

Basilisk lizards are found in Central and South America. The big feet and great speed of this lizard enable it to run across rivers, streams, and ponds. Many of the native peoples of the tropics call it the "Jesus Christ" lizard because of its ability to walk on water. Not only can the Basilisk lizard race on the water, it can run with great speed over the ground and through the treetops, too.

Water Walkers

Think about some of the places you walk—on sidewalks, on the playground, down dirt trails, or through the woods. All of those places are on land. What do you think would happen if you decided to walk on water? You'd quickly sink, that's what!

When we think about organisms that walk, we usually think about creatures that walk over land or through the trees. Few of us would ever think about an animal that walks on water. Yet, the basilisk lizard of Central and South America does just that!

The basilisk lizard lives near ponds and streams in **tropical rain forests** (dense, green forests with lots of rain, mostly in South America). Approximately 2 feet long, it has a large crest that runs from its head down the length of its body. From the side, it looks like an angry dragon. In fact, it was named for an ancient Greek monster that breathed fire and poison. Legends told of how people died after one glance from its fearsome eyes.

When a basilisk lizard is disturbed by an enemy, it drops down from the trees where it lives into the water below. It begins to move its back feet rapidly and, by holding its body semi-erect, is able to run across the surface of the water without falling in. It can do this because its body is lightweight and its hind legs are long and thin and end in toes fringed with scales. Although its back feet look like those of a frog, they are not webbed. Strong muscles help the basilisk move the rear legs so rapidly that the soles of its feet do not break through the water surface when it runs.

After the basilisk has run across the surface of a pond or stream for one to three dozen yards, it begins to slow down and eventually sinks into the water. There, it is able to continue its journey by quickly swimming to the opposite shore.

The ability of the basilisk to run across the surface of water helps it survive in its natural environment. It is also how this amazing animal has learned to adapt to its surroundings.

Snails can be found all over the world but are primarily concentrated in areas where there is a lot of vegetation, moisture, and warm weather. Some of the largest snails can be found in Africa—the African giant snail can grow to a length of nearly 15 inches. These snails spend much of their time eating various plants and fruits, such as bananas. They have also been discovered eating dead animals.

Slimy Slippers

Most of the animals you know have two or four or eight feet. That is, all of their feet come in pairs. You're about to meet an animal that has only one foot and that foot is actually its stomach!

The snail is a most amazing creature. It is one member of a group of animals called **gastropods**, or "bellyfoots." That means that these animals travel around on their stomachs. How would you like to spend the day crawling around on your stomach?

When a snail "walks" it moves by generating a series of waves along the length of its foot. These waves pass from the front to the back of the foot creating a rippling motion. Also, as it moves, the snail gives out a slimy substance from just behind its head. This slime helps it travel over rough surfaces and sharp objects. In fact, a snail can climb over a razor blade without cutting itself! The slime track that the snail creates is not a continuous smear, however, but actually a series of patches where sections of the foot have come in contact with the ground.

Snails like to live in damp places among plants, under stones, or in the soil. They are most active when the weather is wet or moist. In dry weather, snails are often inactive and may attach themselves to a wall or tree trunk and withdraw into their shells for a period of several days or weeks.

This brief period of inactivity is called estivation and is similar to hibernation—the time when snails bury themselves under several inches of soil, slow down their bodily functions, and remain inactive over the cold winter months. In very dry areas or very cold arcas of the world, some snails are able to hibernate for up to four years!

A snail has two sets of tentacles. The upper pair is longer and have "eyes" at the tips. However, a snail cannot see like you can—it can only tell light from dark. The other set of tentacles is much shorter, and they are used to feel objects as the snail walks along. These tentacles are also used to "hear" sounds by detecting vibrations of objects or organisms. Both sets of tentacles can be pulled into the head of the snail whenever it feels threatened or wants to protect itself.

An animal that can walk on one foot! An animal whose one foot is actually its stomach! An animal whose head is on its foot! Truly, the snail is a most amazing walker—one you are sure to discover in your garden or in some nearby woods.

Fantastic Fact

Snails have up to
20,000 little teeth—
all on their tongues.

Pond Patrols

Usually less than 1 inch in length and with a slender body, these long-legged bugs can be found in freshwater areas all over the world. There are about 30 species of water striders in North America.

To find food, to seek a mate, or to escape from their enemies, many animals need to travel from one place to another. To do this, most animals live in specialized locations. One of the more distinctive is an animal that spends most of its life living and walking on the surface of water—water striders.

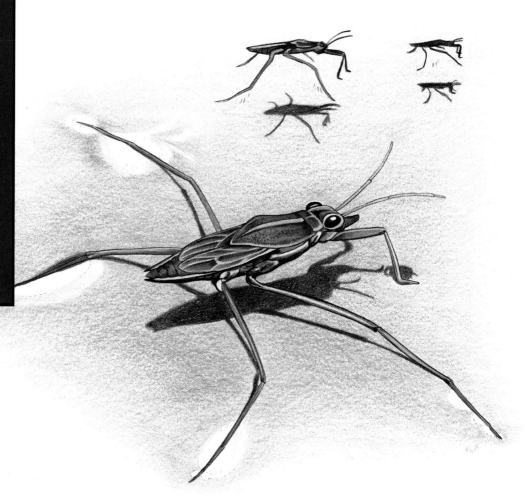

If you have ever visited a pond or looked carefully at a slow-moving stream, you may have seen these creatures darting about on the surface of the water. In fact, these insects are able to run, walk, skip, and hop all over the surface of the water without ever getting wet.

Water striders have three pairs of legs; however, they only use the back four feet when they walk on the water. These two pairs of legs have thick pads of hair on them that repel water and prevent water striders from sinking. The back legs are used to steer water striders across the surface of the water, while the middle legs are used to push them along.

Typically, water striders congregate in large numbers on the surface of the water. Here, they feed on smaller insects or other invertebrates (animal that don't have backbones). Water striders are predatory animals, attacking other creatures and using their sharp piercing mouthparts to suck the body fluids from their prey.

Although water striders can easily walk across the surface of a pond, they are also great runners. They can move at great speeds over the surface of the water. Whole groups of them skipping across the surface of a pond is truly an amazing sight.

Water striders are also known for leaping into the air and landing softly on the surface of the water without getting wet. Unfortunately, all this movement tends to attract the attention of fish who like to sneak up from below to make a tasty meal of these water walkers.

When walking, water striders hold their short front legs up under their heads for balance. Their bodies never touch the water.

The sloth is a mammal found deep in the rain forests of Central and South America. There are seven species of sloths divided into two groups—the two-toed sloths and the three-toed sloths. Two-toed sloths can be found from Honduras to Northern Argentina. Three-toed sloths can be found from Venezuela to Brazil. The two-toed sloth is more common than the three-toed sloth and is the type most often seen in zoos.

Careful Creepers

You have met some animals that can walk on water, others that can walk on their stomachs, and even some animals that can walk with no legs at all! But have you ever met an animal that can walk upside down?

One of the most unusual animals in the world, the sloth spends almost its entire life upside down. The sloth not only walks upside down through the trees, it also sleeps, mates, and gives birth to its babies while it hangs upside down. In fact, sloths may sleep for more than 20 hours a day hanging from the branches of a tree.

A sloth "walks" slowly through a tree and is one of the slowest moving animals in the world. The average "speed" for a sloth is about 4 feet a minute. Many people often refer to something that is slow moving as "slothful."

Sloths belong to the order of animals known as Edentata, which means "without teeth." It was once thought that sloths had no teeth, but they do have a set of black teeth which are difficult to see from a distance. They use these teeth to eat leaves and fruit in the trees where they live.

Sloths hang from the rain forest trees by means of long curved claws that look like meat hooks. Their arms are much longer than their legs and are ideally suited for an upside-down life. Unfortunately, sloths cannot walk upright on their arms and legs. Whenever they are on the ground they must slowly (and painfully) drag themselves to another tree.

Another distinguishing feature of sloths not found in any other animal is the fact that their hair grows from their bellies to their backs. In most mammals, hair grows from the top of the back to the stomach. But because sloths live upside down in a very wet environment, their "opposite-growing" hair allows rainwater to run off. Sloth hair is also covered by a layer of green algae (aquatic plant organisms) which helps conceal them from enemies. Their green color and sluggish habits make sloths look more like masses of dead leaves than living animals.

The enemies of sloths include jaguars and ocelots, as well as the most dangerous enemy of all—humans. The native peoples of the rain forests hunt sloths for their meat. Other people are burning down large sections of rain forests destroying the plants that sloths need to survive. As the rain forest is destroyed, so is the habitat of the sloth. There may come the day when the only sloths alive will be those found in zoos.

Fantastic Fact

The fastest recorded speed for a three-toed sloth is .068 mph—that's only 6 feet per minute!

PROTECTING WEIRD WALKERS

The following groups and organizations have lots of information you can use. Call or write them and ask for material on how you can become involved in preserving plant and animal species around the world.

Save the Rain Forest

604 Jamie Street
Dodgeville, WI 53533
(Raises money to purchase and preserve large tracts of rain forest land and works with native peoples to protect the plants and animals of the rain forest, including sloths, tree frogs, and basilisk lizards.)

National Wildlife Federation

8925 Leesburg Pike
Vienna, VA 22184
(Works to preserve, conserve, and properly manage plant and wildlife resources around the world.)

The animals and plants you read about in this book are examples of organisms with unusual means of locomotion. Their means of travel is a factor in how they are able to survive in a particular environment. Creatures that run fast (basilisk lizards, ostriches) are able to escape from their enemies. Slow-moving animals (sloths, snails) can conserve their energy while locating food.

The ways in which an organism travels through its environment is an example of adaptation—features or behaviors that help an organism survive in a particular environment over a period of years. Organisms adapt to their environments by learning about which foods to eat, who their enemies are, and how to travel through that environment. Adaptation is a process that may take hundreds or thousands of years. It is not something that happens quickly.

Unfortunately, something that does happen quickly is the destruction of certain environments around the world. When humans burn down large sections of the Brazilian rain forest, part of the sloth's environment is endangered. When people drain shorelines and fill them in to build housing developments, part of the mangrove tree's environment is endangered. When farmers spray dangerous chemicals or pesticides on their fields, the millipede's environment is endangered. For many organisms it may have taken hundreds of years to adapt to a particular environment. Yet, that environment can be destroyed or seriously altered in just a few years, resulting in the death or elimination of large numbers of plants and animals.

As you might suspect, humans are the major cause of the extinction of many organisms. The eradication of habitats, the depletion of food sources, and the introduction of foreign species into an area all contribute to this global problem. But that does not mean that we can't all work together to reduce this dilemma.

I invite you to join with your teachers, parents, and friends and work together so that the weird walkers and other inhabitants of this planet will be around for many years and many generations. First of all, take some time to learn about the organisms that live in your part of the world. You may wish to read other books like this one or talk with various adults (such as a high school biology teacher or a college professor) to discover information about the plants and animals native to your area.

Another way you can learn more about various organisms is to visit nearby botanical gardens, zoos, wildlife preserves, aquariums, and arboretums. Be sure to share what you discover with family members and classmates. Also, you may wish to write to various conservation groups (see the list on these pages) and ask them for informational brochures or newsletters. By learning as much as possible and getting involved, we can all help preserve the weird walkers of the world as well as other plants and animals. Together, we can make a difference!

National Audubon Society

666 Pennsylvania Avenue SE
Washington, DC 20003
(A strong advocate of environmental protection, this group helps pass environmental laws, maintains national sanctuaries and nature centers, and conducts a variety of educational programs for adults and kids.)

The Nature Conservancy

1815 N. Lynn Street
Arlington, VA 22209
(Its mission is to purchase selected habitats around the world—thus protecting the plant life and animals that live in those distinctive environments.)

Friends of Wildlife Conservation

New York Zoological Society
185 Street, Southern Blvd.
Bronx Zoo
Bronx, NY 10460
(This group works to ensure the survival of many animals around the world, including several endangered species.)

My Amazing Animal Adventures

The date of my adventure: _____

The people who came with me: _____

_____

Where I went: _____

What amazing animals I saw:

_____   _____

_____   _____

_____   _____

_____   _____

The date of my adventure: _____

The people who came with me: _____

_____

Where I went: _____

What amazing animals I saw:

_____   _____

_____   _____

_____   _____

INTERNET SITES

You can find out more interesting information about all these *Amazing Animals* and lots of other plants and wildlife by visiting these web sites.

http://endangered.fws.gov	U.S. Fish and Wildlife Service
www.animal.discovery.com	Discovery Channel Online
www.kidsplanet.org	Defenders of Wildlife
www.nationalgeographic.com/kids	National Geographic Society
www.nwf.org	National Wildlife Federation
www.ran.org/index.html	Rainforest Action Network
www.tnc.org	The Nature Conservancy
www.worldwildlife.org	World Wildlife Fund

INDEX

Aplomado Falcon, 108

Backswimmers, 78
Basilisk Lizards, 148
Bucket Orchids, 60

Casque-headed Frogs, 20
Chameleons, 12
Cleaner Wrasses, 56
Community Spider, 112

Deep-Sea Vent Organisms, 50
Devil Fish, 88
Dragonfly, 122

Fireflies, 48
Flying Geckos, 26

Gray Whale, 124
Gray Wolf, 120
Great Barracuda, 114
Guillemots, 86

Human Beings, 64
Hydras, 140

Kangaroo Rats, 44
Krill, 80

Ladybird Beetle (Ladybug), 104
Lampreys, 82

Leaf insects, 14
Living Stones, 34

Mangrove Trees, 144
Marine Iguanas, 76
Measuring Worms, 142
Millipedes, 134
Mudskippers, 132

North Pacific Giant Octopus, 106
Nudibranchs, 42

Orchid Praying Mantises, 22
Ostriches, 138

Pipefish, 16
Pitcher Plant,116
Poison Arrow Frogs, 62
Polar Bears, 52
Ptarmigans, 30
Puffer Fish, 92
Purple Sea Snails, 90

Saltwater Crocodile, 110
Sargassum Fish, 32
Scallops, 84
Sea Dragons, 24
Sea Otters, 94
Sea Snakes, 74
Servals, 18

Siphonophore, 118
Sloths, 154
Snails, 150
Snakes, 58
Squids, 72
Starfish, 146
Strangler Figs, 46

Tiger, 102
Tree Frogs, 136

Walking Sticks, 28
Water Striders, 152
Weaver Ants, 54